Shades of My Mother

Shades of My Mother

Moving Beyond That Reflection

NANCY DESCOTEAUX CULOS

To my mother, Catherine Carroll Descoteaux,
without whom I would never have been able to even imagine
a life of personal and professional freedom
and independence. She didn't tell me what to do; she showed me how
to do it despite the gender-based obstacles in her path.

George R. Villa, the president of Uniroyal and
my mother's boss for forty years,
summed her up best at her retirement in 1986 when he said,
"If Kay Descoteaux were a man, I would've been working for her."

Table of Contents

Introduction

For some obscure reason, I've always talked about writing a book. Possibly because my mother always said she should write a book, but no one would believe her story. She may have been right. Would someone believe that my father once drove by our house, hit my aunt's car parked there, and kept going? My mother and my aunt were sitting in the living room, and my aunt said incredulously, "I think Dick just drove by, hit my car, and kept going." Or the time the husband of a woman my father was having an affair with came to our house to confront him and confronted my mother instead. Who would even believe she stayed with my father for over fifty years, but she did. But I'm getting ahead of myself.

Writing, for me, was one of those things that I talked about but was too busy or too undisciplined to sit down and really apply myself to until the dreaded COVID-19 pandemic struck. Then, all we had was time—and time literally stood still. The routines of daily life, like going to work and getting together with friends and family, became dangerous "super spreaders" and were replaced by virtual events. Out of boredom bordering on ennui, I enrolled in a Zoom memoir writing class, and thus it began. The first assignment was to write about a defining moment in your life, something you thought changed the trajectory of your life.

I wrote about the most defining and terrifying moment of my life. The words flowed freely like a mountain stream because I had journaled every day for two years during that period of my life. I knew if I didn't write it down, no one would believe it, just like my mother's old fear. While I knew I would include that defining moment somewhere in my memoir, ultimately I decided not to start my story there. But as I was rereading my journals, I came across an entry I had written about my mother when I was forty-one years old, newly divorced, and working full-time. In it, I reflected on my mother who was about to retire after a long successful career in business.

I had written about how I felt when I was a preteen and always wondered to myself: *Why does my mother have to work? None of the other mothers in the neighborhood work. They're all home for lunch and after school. Why?* I felt angry and cheated, and my often-sulky attitude communicated that to my mother loudly and clearly enough to make her feel guilty about her choice. She acknowledged that she carried that guilt with her for many years. Realizing that was a profound moment for me.

It dawned on me that my mother's going off to work in 1946 when I was five years old, with two younger siblings and another to come within a year, was the most defining moment in my life. I could see what courage and determination that took for her to do this when there was no one fighting for her rights—no Abzug, Friedan, or Steinem yet. I realize she went to work because main-taining home and hearth were not enough for her intellectually; it wasn't her "thing." I've realized that my story, my struggles, and my successes are attributable to her and what she conveyed to me by her actions—and what my father conveyed to me by his reactions. I don't know if he supported her emotionally, but I did see a man cook, do laundry, take care of kids, and make his own lunches. He was a man who played ball with me, took me ice skating and golfing, and expected me to do what any boy could do and do it well.

So, I decided to start my story where my career began, the defining moment when I decided what I wanted to be when I grew up. This memoir is about my life's journey, the choices I made, and the choices I didn't make because of the influence and example of both my parents and their support of me to become the best I could be as a woman.

Part One

The Foundation

Chapter 1

The Path Is Chosen

In 1958, my father was in the hospital having his spine fused because of a ruptured disc. I was a junior in high school, and every day after school, I walked across the street from my all-girls Catholic school to the Catholic hospital to visit him. During these visits, I'd see the young, sharp nurses in crisp, white uniforms—so efficient, but so caring and helpful. The old, dull nurses had advanced to management positions. I learned about them a little later in my journey.

The nurses appeared to command respect just by their presence. It was probably because the patients were at their mercy. Also, I'm embarrassed to admit, my vanity kicked in. I knew I'd look good in a crisp white uniform. I was sixteen years old.

Really, what would you expect!

I thought, *Maybe I should be a nurse.* Jo, my best friend then and for the next fifty years of our lives, had always wanted to be a nurse, so there was that, too, though her motivation was less self-serving than mine. Her mother, an OB/GYN nurse, had died giving birth to her, leaving a five-year-old son, a three-year-old daughter, and Jo, a newborn. Jo carried this loss throughout her life. There were no nurses in my family, so I had no idea of what I was in for.

All through high school, I thought I wanted to go to Katherine Gibbs Secretarial School in New York City or become an English teacher when I graduated. The first career choice was probably because my mother worked in Manhattan for many years as the executive secretary of the president of Uniroyal when they relocated from Naugatuck, Connecticut, to New York City in 1956. She'd take the train down to the city on Mondays and come back home on Fridays. In New York, she stayed at the Barbizon Hotel for Women. From the time I was thirteen or fourteen years old, I often met my mother in New York City for shopping or to go to a play. Her work always seemed exciting to me, and I thought maybe that's what I could do, when I grew up. The English teacher bit was just because I loved grammar, literature, and writing, and it came easy to me. In my teen years, easy mattered to me. I didn't take "the road less traveled." I don't think many teenagers do. They usually travel the same roads their friends are traveling. But my father's hospitalization planted a very different seed.

Up to that point, I always had a summer job in the layaway department of Worth's Department Store in Waterbury, which was like the modern-day Macy's. My best friend Joyce and I got the jobs because her mother worked for Mr. Greenberg, the store's president and founder. It was a fun job. We got a 15 percent discount on purchases—I always bought clothes—and we got to cover the switchboard while the person who really knew what they were doing went to lunch. The switchboard was like the one Lily Tomlin did her operator routine on the television show *Laugh-In* in the late 1960s. With all those wires and plugs, you have no idea what a mess you can make of it—the kind that makes you start giggling and then you can't stop. It nearly got me fired once.

Joyce and I would cover the switchboard together. We'd answer, "Worth's Smiling Service! How can I help you?" One day, the caller happened to be S.H. Greenberg, the store's owner, and we managed to disconnect him. We didn't get fired, but we never covered the switchboard together again.

That wasn't the first time Joyce and I got in trouble over phone calls. One day, when we were probably ten or eleven years old, we were playing at Joyce's house, which I was happy about because she was an only child. She had so many games, and they always had all the pieces. In my house, that was not the case. She could always find the key to our roller skates too. That was another rarity in a house with four kids and a working mother. An added bonus of being at Joyce's house was not being around my younger brother and sisters.

One day, we got it into our heads to call in to the *Ted Mack Amateur Hour*, a talent show on television where we could vote for our favorite acts. We didn't think twice about calling until Joyce's mother got the phone bill with all the long distance calls on it and went crazy. Of course, then Joyce and I blamed it on each other.

The next summer after my dad's hospitalization, I didn't go back to Worth's for a job but instead got one as a nurse's aide at St. Mary's Hospital in Waterbury. I can't describe what I loved about it. I wasn't in white; I was dressed in pink. There was some scut work, but it was very interesting dealing with the patients, their families, the doctors, the nurses—and the misery as well as the hope.

Hospitals in the late 1950s had no ICUs (Intensive Care Units), so the sickest of patients were in the wards with the not-so-sick ones. That summer, I worked on an all-male unit of four-, six-, and eight-bed rooms. (Only wealthy patients had private rooms then.) On that job, I moved back and forth between medical and surgical units where the patients were of all ages. That included handsome young men who were flirty, cranky old men who were miserable, and lecherous middle-aged men you didn't want to get too close to. Then there were the malnourished, yellow-skinned alcoholics in the DTs, shackled to their beds and receiving intravenous fluids of glucose with Berroca C injected into it. That fluid was the most awful-smelling yellow stuff, with an indescribable odor you'd never forget. It also stained your hands.

There also were amputees still sensing their lost limbs and crying out from the phantom pain. There were patients with every type of cancer at a time when all cancers were incurable, essentially a death sentence. Cutting the cancer out or off was the only solution. Some poor souls had radical neck surgery for throat cancer which involved removing their tracheas and half their jaws, leaving lifelong disfigurement and a permanent hole in their neck to breathe through. They often didn't live much longer, and their quality of life was questionable.

But I loved it. It was never boring and always rewarding because I was always busy, and the time flew by. I detest being bored to this day. I learned quickly and was unusually responsible for a teen, so the nurses liked it when I was working with them. They were always willing to take the time to teach me something new, because I made their jobs easier most of the time . . . but not always.

Once, while cleaning a patient's denture, I dropped it down the hopper sink that was meant for bedpans and shouldn't have been using to clean dentures. We had to call the maintenance guy to take the sink apart and get the teeth out of the drain. The nurse wasn't too happy with me, and the poor guy probably wondered why it took me forty minutes to clean his dentures. I'll never forget him. He had had a heart attack and constantly complained of chest pain, even after getting pain medication. The nurses thought he was exaggerating until one morning, when I got to the unit, I found out he had died during the night. I never took a patient's complaint of pain for granted after that. Ever.

That summer, I decided to become a nurse, and no one was more shocked than my mother.

"Honey," she said, "you passed out when your brother sliced his finger. What are you thinking?"

I don't think I really knew what I was thinking. Fortunately, I was classically prepared in high school, having studied the sciences, two languages, and advanced math. Sure, I couldn't type but I could think critically and problem-solve. Without those two skills, I would have really struggled in nursing. But making the decision to go into nursing was certainly another of the most defining moments of my life. It really set the trajectory for my career, my marriage, my divorce, and my life's work. Nursing was the thread that wound through my entire adult life.

While my father's hospitalization was the impetus for the decision, without who my mother was, how she became that person, and the faith she had in me, my success in life would not have been guaranteed.

But it wasn't easy as it sounds! This is how I made it happen.

Chapter 2

The Incidental Trendsetter

My mother, *Catherine Carroll*, was the oldest of three born to Irish immigrants in 1918. Her mother, Mariah O'Brien, emigrated to the United States from Ireland by herself, leaving parents, sisters, brothers in Spa Tralee, County Kerry. I only wish I knew why my grandmother came here and how she did it. I know one thing for sure: She hated the English "devils," as she called them. When she was born in 1882, Ireland was governed by the English, and although the potato famine had ended thirty years earlier in 1852, the impact of one million Irishmen dying and a million more forced to leave their homes was surely felt for many years after.

My grandmother, whom I called Nana, landed in Haverhill, Boston, around 1912 and worked in a rectory there doing housekeeping and cooking for priests. Somehow she ended up in Waterbury, Connecticut, married to my grandfather, Jeremiah Carroll, who I called Pop. He, too, had emigrated to the states alone from County Cork, Ireland. They married when my grandmother was thirty-five years old, late in life for even those times, and had three children: my mother, Catherine, the oldest; my Aunt Ceil; and my Uncle Buddy.

My mother always told me how high-strung and stern Nana was and hinted that she had a nervous breakdown while going through menopause. Nana was especially tough with her, setting high expectations, especially academically, for her oldest daughter. I believe all first-generation immigrant women were tough. There was no option but to fight for yourself and your family against terrible odds.

My mother would often tell me she had an inferiority complex growing up. Her younger sister, Cecile, was considered the beauty with her blue eyes and curly blond hair, and a flirty personality and an ego to go with her looks. Those looks and attitude got her into trouble more than once. It was serious trouble when she got pregnant at seventeen and was sent off to stay with cousins in Bridgeport so she could carry the baby to term and then give up a healthy baby boy for adoption. My Uncle Buddy, of course, was just plain spoiled, being the youngest and a boy.

My mother was a classic beauty with hazel eyes and auburn hair. She also had great legs that were the envy of Cecile, who had "piano legs" (the term my mother used). Catherine Carroll wasn't only a pretty face; she was also the smartest kid in her class. In every class from elementary through high school, she was always first. She was as serious as her sister was frivolous. When she graduated as high school valedictorian, she was awarded full scholarships to two colleges: Trinity and Catholic University in Washington, DC. I don't know exactly why she didn't go to either, but perhaps because it was so unusual and out-of-the-ordinary for women to pursue higher education at that time in history. Still, not continuing in school proved to be a defining moment in her life and for the family she was to have.

CATHERINE CARROLL

The very tilt of her nose, the quirk of her lips, and the care-free laugh—tell us that our "Kay" is a colleen in the true sense of the word. And yet, it is not mischief alone that lurks in those sparkling blue eyes. For we who have worked and played with "Kay" during the four years of our high school careers, know that there is a serious side to her nature which is proven by her scholastic achievments. It is inevitable that "Kay" will succeed with such rare talents as she possesses.

Catherine was so serious that she thought she would be a nun and didn't think motherhood was for her—and in the traditional sense, it wasn't. In another sense, she was the perfect mother. She did nothing but praise and love each one of her children in a special way so my siblings and I grew up to be positive, confident, and self-assured. All she ever asked of us was to love and respect one another. I don't think there is a greater gift a mother can give her child.

My mother gave me another priceless gift. The nontraditional path she took after having her kids gave me a real advantage when advantages for women in the business world were almost nonexistent. My mother role-modeled for me that a woman could carve out a career for herself despite the obstacles. She went from carpooling to Naugatuck Chemical, where she worked as a payroll clerk, to being driven in a limo to a building on Sixth Avenue in New York City to work for the president of the then United States Rubber Company (later Uniroyal)—dressed in a pants suit, no less. When I was growing up, there were no other women in my universe who dressed that way. Any inferiority my mother felt personally was replaced with pride in what she accomplished.

While my mother had a career that paved the way for my later success as an adult, I tortured her with guilt through my preteen years for not being at home when most mothers were. She wasn't there making cupcakes for a bake sale at school or mending our socks. She wasn't there when we got home from school, something my younger brother and sisters seemed to be unaware of—or perhaps I was unduly aware. I remember playing outside until dusk, and then, knowing she'd be home soon, I'd walk down to the corner to meet her.

As she stepped out of her friend's car, she'd ask, "Honey, where's your brother?" (She always called me "Honey.") That question quickly would be followed by, "Did you peel the potatoes?"

I didn't like being the one responsible for my younger siblings until she got home, and I made it known. I was sulky and could be miserable. She would often say she knew I was unhappy with her as a mother and didn't think she always did what I thought was the right thing. Fortunately, when I was old enough to understand what she did and why, I was able to have a conversation with her and not only apologize but also thank her for being a different kind of mother for the times.

The Carroll/Descoteaux Wedding

If my mother had gone off to Catholic University instead of going to work in Scovill's pin shop, she never would've met Harold "Dick" Descoteaux. The youngest of nine, he had lost his father when he was a young boy and his mother when he was seventeen. He had quit school and gone to work when he was eighteen to help the family out. I believe my mom met him one day when she and my Aunt Ceil and their girlfriends went to a St. Anne's Athletic Club baseball game at Hamilton Park. My mother had classmate friends from other Catholic parishes like St. Anne's since Sacred Heart was the only Catholic secondary school in the city.

When my parents met, my mother was eighteen, and my father was twenty-one. They dated for three years before they were married. Something that should have been a harbinger of things to come: My father cheated on my mother with her sister Ceil when she and my father were engaged, but the wedding still went on.

Supposedly opposites attract, but there's a limit to how many differences can be overcome in any relationship. Whatever the attraction was, my parents dated seriously and became engaged, in spite of my grandmother's resistance to the idea. Ethnic prejudices were as strong then as now, but now the ethnicities were different. Nana was not happy with a "pea-soup" (a derogatory name for a Frenchman) joining the family. Because of that prejudice, my father was not allowed in my grandmother's house when they were dating. That meant he and my mother would have to meet on the corner of William Street and East Main Street whenever they went out together.

Harold Francis Descoteaux and Catherine Mary Carroll were married November 16, 1940, in Sacred Heart Church by Father Blansfield. Nine months and three days later, I was born on August 19, 1941. Five months later, on December 7, 1941, the Japanese bombed Pearl Harbor, and the United States entered World War II.

From the very start, my parents couldn't agree on the simplest of things—for example, my name. My father would joke around and say, "Let's call her Esmerelda." The nuns in the hospital didn't think it was so funny and finally told my mother she had to choose a name so they could complete the birth certificate. My father was not around—probably out golfing—so my mother told her my name was Cecilia Mary, after her sister. When my dad came to visit her that night, she told him.

The Carroll-Descoteaux wedding. Aunt Ciel, Uncle Buddy, Mom and Dad. 1940

His response: "That's not what I wanted to name her. I wanted to name her Anita and call her Nancy."

Her response: "Well, it's too late now."

We know now how that ended. I've been called Nancy ever since except in school, where I was always Cecilia. The only entities that know me as Cecilia now are Medicare and Social Security.

The timing of my birth, nine months and three days after my parents got married, was a definite indication that my mother had no clue about birth control and, being an Irish Catholic, chose not to learn. My father, being a passionate Frenchman, wasn't apt to abstain, resulting in four more kids in the next five years. That made me the oldest of five, not necessarily a burden but definitely a responsibility that made a significant impact on who I was and how I managed my life. Having five children also kept my father from being drafted to fight in World War II, a conflict that would last four more years after my birth.

I don't consciously remember much before I was four or five, but being the firstborn, those early years from birth to three were so well documented with photos individually captioned and catalogued in albums that I count them as memories.

The captions read: *Nancy's first smile, Nancy's first steps, Nancy's first words, first pet, first Christmas, first snowman.* My siblings would remark ad nauseum about that through the years.

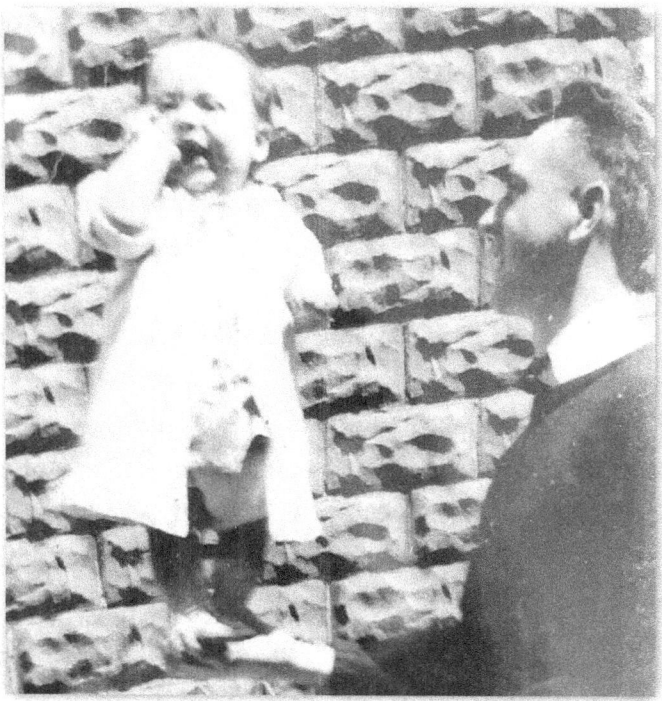

Standing on Dad's hand and loving it

But, yes, there were pictures of my first birthday, dressed in a fancy white dress, with patent leather shoes and lacy socks, and holding a beautiful corsage of roses my father gave me. There were also photos of me at every age from toddler to teen, sitting on the front steps of our house with every kid on the street. None of my siblings had that kind of photographic record to claim for themselves. For years to come, my brother and sisters were quick to remind me: "You were always the favorite!"

I had a brother Ricky born ten months after me, but he never came home from the hospital. My mother said that when they arrived home that day with no baby, my father picked me up, his firstborn, took me into their bedroom, and closed the door, crying. Many years later my mother told me that Ricky was an Rh factor baby, which caused him to be completely jaundiced. His blood type and my mother's were not compatible. She told me that a transfusion from my father would have saved him, but he was on the golf course, and they couldn't get to him in time. No cell phones, remember. By the time she told me this story, their marriage was on very shaky ground, and her bitterness was always there. The marriage stayed rife with resentment until they both passed. They tormented each other relentlessly, particularly after they were both retired and were home all day together—that is, when they spoke to each other at all.

As a youngster, I had no idea that my parents' marriage wasn't a match made in heaven. There were no raging battles, not even any harsh words. My mother always avoided confrontation, regardless of the situation. I remember one time, though, when I was fourteen—my father's current girlfriend's husband came to our house looking for my father and gave my mother a black eye by mistake. That's when I knew the state of the marriage and didn't wonder any more. But this didn't affect how I felt about my father.

I wouldn't say I idolized him, but I was always very close to him. I felt that I was more like him than my mother, and I was in many ways, not just in looks. My mother was smart, and I got her brains, but she never cared if the closets were organized, the kitchen counter was cleared, or the oven was clean. She wasn't a slob, but my father was fastidious. His closet and drawers were perfectly organized, with every pair of shoes, including his golf shoes, polished and in shoe trees. He was the one who made us put our stuff away, wash and dry the dishes, close the door, shut off the lights, and pick up our feet. Even as a teenager, I was always organizing and cleaning not only my room, but also the whole house and doing the laundry. I was also blessed with my father's athleticism, love of physical activity, and competitive spirit. There were no formal sports programs for women at that time, but I was a tomboy and could compete with the boys in the neighborhood, where there was always something going on in the street or at the nearby parks.

Chapter 3

Early Years

We lived in a working-class Waterbury neighborhood at 98 Lounsbury Street, one of the many side streets off Baldwin Street, lined with three-family houses on both sides. The houses were basically the same, other than the color of paint. They all had sidewalks from back to front, postage-stamp-sized backyards with little or no grass, and front porches. The room layouts inside were the same. Our first-floor rental had a kitchen with a pantry, a dining room, and a living room—all in a line from back to front with one bedroom off the kitchen, one bedroom off the dining room, and a bathroom in between. There was also a small foyer off the living room; that's where the telephone table with the big, black dial phone sat.

We had a party line, which meant that at least three families had the same phone line with different rings for each number—and yes, you could listen in on other conversations if you were really quiet. Ours was two short rings. The number was Plaza 43738 with Plaza later becoming 75. The technological changes over my lifetime are dizzying and unbelievable to my grandchildren, who have no clue that phones used to be attached to the wall. My maternal grandparents, Nana and Pop, lived on the third floor of that house. I'm not sure how that came to be, but the close proximity to them greatly influenced the rest of my life in a hundred positive ways.

Growing up in the 1950s was uneventful, at least in our neighborhood. The war was over, the economy was good, and there seemed to be jobs for everyone in our city. I do remember hearing vague threats of nuclear war from the Russian Communists, or "the Reds," as they were called, and there were pretend air raids. The sirens would go off and we would run for cover, or if we were in school, we would get under our desks and cover our heads. I don't think any of that would have saved us if the Russians had decided to drop an atom bomb, but the local Civil Defense League thought it was a good idea to keep practicing.

I've always thought of myself as growing up middle-class, but Waterbury was really a factory city, known as the "Brass Center of the World." There were many rolling mills and factories: American Brass, Scovill Manufacturing (my father and grandfather both worked there), Chase Brass and Copper, the Waterbury Buckle Company, and Naugatuck Chemical. Years later, the Chemical became part of the United States Rubber Company, or US Rubber, which then became Uniroyal in 1961. It was one of the twelve companies that made up the Dow Industrial Average in 1996.

It was the presence of Naugatuck Chemical that became an important factor in my life. When I was about five years old, my exceedingly intelligent and seriously intellectual mother decided she was going to work. I wish I had asked her years later more about what she was thinking and feeling when she made that decision. I can't imagine it was easily made, and I know it could not have been done without a battle. My father must have been crazed when she talked about going to work. Women didn't work then, especially a woman with four kids under five years of age. My mother wasn't a rebel or a woman's libber before her time, yet I can imagine what drove her to make that choice. My father, typical of men in the 1950s, believed it was a man's world and women were in it just to take care of everyone.

He had a good job at Scovill Manufacturing, so I know my mother's plan to go to work at that time wasn't about the money. But since my father worked in the rod mill on the second shift, he was home in the mornings. I remember that because, weather permitting, he golfed every Saturday, many Sundays, and sometimes in the mornings before he went to work. His friend would pick him up, and off he'd go. There were always drinks after golf, so he rarely came home sober—not drunk but not sober either. That usually meant a nap on the couch.

So, my mother was left with a bunch of kids most of the day, as were most mothers at that time. We didn't have a car until 1953,

Me, David, Kathy and Jerilyn. 1949

so to get anywhere, my mother had to walk or haul three kids and a stroller on the bus to go downtown where the stores were and the only place to shop. If she wanted to go anywhere else in the city, she had to get a transfer for the next bus. Thus, every outing was an all-day affair—not so easy with four kids.

She probably felt like she was losing herself. She wasn't the "Betty-Home-Bake"-type, and she sure as hell wasn't a housekeeper.

What I distinctly remember is that her books were all over the place, and she always had a jigsaw puzzle she was working on spread out on the card table. She did try the "Betty-Home-Bake" route—she sewed, knitted, crocheted, and God knows what else to challenge her mind. This was a woman who, even in her seventies when she couldn't fall asleep, could recite the states and all their capitals in alphabetical order. I'm sure she was totally bored despite having two kids in diapers. The good thing was she would rather read to us than vacuum. Thanks to her packed bookcase, I read many books I probably shouldn't have read until I was a little older. I don't think it hurt me, but I would read anything I could get my hands on, including the *Books of Knowledge* encyclopedia which she purchased from a door-to-door salesman for a dollar down and a dollar a week. I'm sure it was the only sale he made in our neighborhood that day. She also bought a very expensive Electrolux vacuum from a traveling salesman. She was a sucker for a sales pitch!

I wish I could remember more about how logistically it came to be that she went to work. Did she know someone who worked there? How did she arrange a ride to and from work every day? Now there's no one left to ask. She started working at Naugatuck Chemical around 1946. I know it was that year because my youngest sister was born in 1948, and my mother sometimes referred to her as the "Chemical Baby." Having Nana and Pop on the third floor probably made it workable. They were built-in babysitters from the time my father went to work at two o'clock in the afternoon until my mother came home at five o'clock in the evening.

Jerilyn, the Chemical Baby, was her last one. My mother finally wised up and went to the "not-Catholic" hospital across town and had her by Caesarean section and had a hysterectomy at the same time. She was twenty-nine years old. That couldn't have happened in the Catholic hospital, and it was the only dependable birth control back then. I'm sure there was some "diagnosis" that was attached to the surgery to soothe all the Catholic consciences involved, but my mother told me the true story. She took her maternity leave and was back to work in six weeks. How she did it is beyond me, but my father surely deserved some of the credit. I remember that he cooked for us when we came home for lunch before he went to work at 2:30 p.m. I can picture him washing clothes in the double sink and hanging out the laundry, including diapers, before he went to work. My mother told me that the neighborhood women said he had the "whitest whites" on the clothesline. There probably weren't any other fathers in the neighborhood doing housekeeping chores because their wives were home with the kids. My father also made the best lemony iced tea and delicious homemade root beer, sterilizing the bottles and then capping them with rubber stoppers that clamped closed.

At that point in my life, we were a family of six in a rental with two bedrooms and one bath. That left one bedroom for me, David, and Kathy, with Jerilyn in a crib. We had bunk beds, but it was still a tight squeeze. Somehow, because of the cramped conditions, it was decided that I would stay upstairs with Nana and Pop, at least to sleep. I'm sure my mother asked me if I would like that, and of course I said yes. What I remember best about staying upstairs was not unpleasant in the least.

Nana's Kitchen

Nana's kitchen was typical for the times. It had a small white enamel table where she rolled out pastry dough for the most delicious blueberry pies ever. It also had a large gas stove where she made bacon and eggs every morning for my Uncle Buddy, who lived with her ever since he came home from serving in the Army during World War II.

The room also had a big coal-fired stove to heat the apartment.

I loved Nana's kitchen for so many reasons. My Nana, Mariah O'Brien Carroll, was one of those reasons. A stocky Irish woman with hair as white as snow, I can still picture her wiping her strong hands on the apron that she seemed to always wear over her house dress. She used those hands to wash her sheets in the kitchen sink, even when she was ninety years old and living in senior housing. Strong hands, strong woman! She outlived my grandfather, Pop, by thirty years and passed away at 104. My mother used to say Pop was in heaven praying she would have a long life on earth because she didn't give him a minute's peace when he was alive. She wasn't easy, even on me.

She called me "Soupy" because I looked more French than Irish—like my father, the French "pea-soup." I had his brown eyes and dark brown, almost black, poker-straight hair. To her blue Irish eyes, looking like that wasn't a good thing.

In those days, every ethnic group that immigrated to the United States had a pejorative nickname. None are politically correct now. The French were called "pea-soups," though my father never made pea soup in his life.

Nana wasn't thrilled when my mother married this "pea-soup," but she didn't hold who my father was against me and always took loving care of me. She might've washed my face rather harshly and

Mom and Nana cutting the cake on her Hundredth birthday.

been a little rough when she braided my hair, but I never felt anything but love from her.

The second and most compelling reason I loved Nana's kitchen was because my Pop would also be there. Jeremiah Carroll was a tall, slim, blue-eyed sweet Irishman, who, when he wasn't working in Scovill's Steel Mill or walking to Paul's package store for a quart of Ballantine Ale, sat in the kitchen by the window in his rocking chair, smoking his pipe, and listening to the radio. In the summer, it was the Boston Red Sox baseball games. He hated the "Damn Yankees." He always wore a collared white shirt, a vest, and a brimmed cap. Pop was as amiable and sweet as Nana was prickly and tough. I can still physically feel the warmth in that kitchen, and it wasn't from the big coal stove. It was from my Pop, who was easy with me and never denied me anything.

I got to sleep at Nana's in the dining room on the studio couch. We'd call it a daybed today. I wasn't unhappy there—on the contrary, I felt safe and sheltered, and I don't remember ever wishing to be anywhere else. In the evening, I listened to the radio with Pop—shows like *Amos and Andy, Fibber McGee and Molly*—and when I was in bed, I could hear the creaking door of *Inner Sanctum* and laughter from *The Jack Benny Show* with Rochester. My favorite radio show was *The Life of Riley*.

Nana made sure I was fed breakfast and dressed for school. I never really liked the plaid

Pop and me

dresses she made me wear. I didn't like the braids in my hair either, so I'd take them out as I walked to school. When I got home, she would "raise rim" (her expression) or be angry at me for taking out the braids or getting my dress dirty, but I still felt the love from her. And Pop, well, he made sure I had a "sup of orange soda" when Nana said there wasn't any, and I got my share of the butterscotch candies that always filled the candy dish on the buffet in the dining room.

Until I began sleeping upstairs with Nana, all four of us stayed in the same ten-by-twelve-foot room. When we were little, we were all put to bed at the same time, and of course there was giggling, jumping from one bed to another, and fighting. My brother, David, was in the top bunk, and Kath and Jerilyn (who we sometimes called "Jer") were at opposite ends of the bottom bunk. I was in the single bed across the room. No one went right to sleep. My mother would threaten that she was going to come in and we'd be sorry, but those were only threats. Then my father would say, "I'm coming in!" and he meant it, as he took off his belt. We'd be cowering then, because we knew someone was going to get it. We'd be pleading, "It wasn't me! It wasn't me!"

I don't know if he swung that belt randomly, but it always seemed that David got the worst of it. We would all cry, but he was the only one who felt the belt.

I don't know how everything fit in that one room. There was one small closet and a large bureau. I have no idea where everyone's clothes were kept, but I do remember a kids' table with four little chairs and many toys and books scattered all over the place. I played with my siblings for hours in that room. When we pretended and played like we were at school, I was always the teacher. When we played store with a small toy cash register and fake coins, I ran the store. I always seemed to be the "grown-up" taking charge over my younger siblings.

Chapter 4

A Memory Reawakened

Children's lives were simpler back then than they are now, but even as I write this, I know that kids in our neighborhood were being abused physically at home. Many things changed over the decades, but sadly those base instincts have stayed the same.

Across the street from our three-family house, in between two other three-family houses, was a tiny, white, somewhat dilapidated single-family house. Benign-looking from the outside, it had a white picket fence with a gate to the sidewalk that surrounded it, and there were red and white rosebushes along the fence in the yard. What went on inside that house wasn't so benign, and I know that even though I never stepped foot in that house. There were five houses on each side of our street, and I had been in every one of those houses, but never in that one.

I knew the kids, Dickie and Peggy, who lived in that house. They were among the twelve or so kids in the neighborhood who were around the same age, and we all played in the street almost every day. Dickie and Peggy played with us most of the time, but not always. They were both so very quiet and seemed very serious. They weren't ragtag, but you could tell they pretty much had to care for themselves. They lived with their grandfather, old Mr. Kelly, and their mother and father. Their mother was also very quiet and wasn't seen much. She and the kids all looked ghostly pale. I can see their father staggering up the street, scowling and red-faced. He was the only one not quiet or ghostly pale. When he was home, the kids weren't allowed out, and you could hear screaming and yelling coming from inside. Sometimes you wouldn't see the kids or their mother for a few days after the screaming and yelling stopped. I would notice my mother and other mothers looking sadly and sympathetically at those kids, especially Dickie. I never saw the violence, but I sensed it. There was no mandatory reporting of child abuse in those days, no school nurses checking young bodies for bruises or burns. There were just whispered accusations and impotent silence.

When I was thirteen, we moved from this neighborhood, so I lost track of Dickie and Peggy—until 1960, when I was in nursing school. I was on the surgical unit and noticed a name on one of the charts: Richard Kelly. His diagnosis was ulcerative colitis, an autoimmune disease, exacerbated by stress. He was in the room we called "the porch" with three other patients. I went in to look, and in the first bed on the left was a weak, pale, frail young man with the blankets pulled up to his chin. His body hardly made a bulge in the bed. He was wide-eyed and looked terrified.

"Hi, Dickie. How are you?" I called out to him.

He slowly turned his head toward me. And I knew by looking at him how sick and deathly ill he was.

"Nancy Descoteaux!" he exclaimed. "Wow, do you work here?" His eyes brightened. I was glad I stopped, but I was heartsick at what I was seeing.

"Yes. I'm a nursing student. How are you doing?"

"Not so good. I can't eat or drink anything." He could barely talk.

"I just wanted to say hello. Do you need anything?"

"No thanks, but I'm glad to see you." He was starting to doze off, so I ended the conversation with, "I'll stop to see you tomorrow."

I knew there were no treatments or cures for ulcerative colitis then. It could be managed somewhat with diet, but the stress also had to be managed or the flare-ups could be deadly.

I went back to see Dickie the next day. When I walked into the room, the first bed on the left was freshly made and empty. I knew immediately that Richard Kelly, the same age as me, had passed. That moment took my breath away and put a little hole in my heart. I wonder whether anyone had ever stepped up and helped this gentle young man cope with the pain and misery he endured in his very short life. To this day, my heart aches for him.

The Neighborhood

Life had not been simple or long for Dickie, but for most of us on Lounsbury Street, our lives were uncomplicated and unfettered by the pressures of "helicopter mothers" and worries about getting on a waiting list for preschool. In fact, there were only experimental helicopters in the 1950s, and there was no preschool. In those days, preschool was being with our family, our neighbors, and playing games in the street with our friends. The street was where we learned to count, to share, to be inclusive, to cooperate and defend ourselves. We learned to negotiate. We learned to move around our neighborhood—on foot, on roller skates, on a bike, and by the time we were ten or eleven, on the city bus. We also learned that boys were sometimes mean, and girls could be cruel.

The games we played then are now lost to history. There was always a chalk-drawn hopscotch game in the street where sides would be drawn for dodgeball, baseball, red light-green light, hide-and-seek, and Double Dutch jump rope. We played outside with all the kids until dark and our mothers had to call us over and over to come inside for the night.

Everyone knew the paper boy and always gave him a tip. The milkman came every third day, clinking glass milk bottles that had cream at the top. There was also a breadman, a rag man (the first recycler), and the man on the vegetable truck, the first "farm-to-table." There was also a guy who sharpened scissors and knives. I think he was a gypsy.

In Waterbury in the 1950s, neighborhoods were more than the street you lived on. They were communities with neighborhood churches, schools, and more. The stores you shopped in were neighborhood stores. Sam's Cleaners and Tailor was on the street level of a three-family house, as was Simpson's Butcher Shop, one block up from Sam's.

Two brothers owned the butcher shop; one was always smiling and the other wasn't. Both wore white aprons on which they wiped their bloody hands when someone came into the store. They could've all been Sweeney Todd, for all I knew. The number of times I walked to that store for my mother or my grandmother must be in the hundreds. The usual list was a loaf of bread, a pound of American cheese sliced thin, a pound of bologna, and a half-pound of liverwurst or blood pudding for my mother. Being the oldest, I ran a lot of errands and sometimes had to drag along a sister or brother—usually a sister. My brother was not so easy to drag along. David never did anything the easy way in spite of being as smart as a whip and athletically gifted.

Paul's Package Store was on the corner across the street from Sam's. I never went there, but my grandfather did often to buy a quart of Ballantine Ale in a green bottle. Bernie's Drug Store was the place to get prescriptions filled, but it also had a soda counter on the left with chrome stools and red leather seat tops. We could get a malt or milkshake while we waited if our mothers gave us enough money. And of course, there were neighborhood bars. A couple of them, Hogan's and McGrath's between our street and the school, were always busy. They were Irish-owned bars—the Harps had a reputation to maintain. There were even two doctors down the hill who practiced in their homes. They didn't live in a three-family house like the rest of us; they had their own homes. We thought they were rich.

We could walk everywhere we needed to go—to the neighborhood movie theater or even downtown to the center which was at the intersection of the city. To this day, bucolic country roads and lanes do not appeal to me. Give me sidewalks and the cityscape like the ones I grew up in any day.

Everyone I knew growing up in Waterbury lived in one of four sections of the city. There was the East End, mostly Irish; the West End, again mostly Irish; the North End, which was Italian and African American; and the South End, which was French. I grew up on Washington Hill between the East and South End. Thinking back, where I grew up was really a mixed bag of cultures—many Irish, but also French, Italian, Albanian, English, Polish, and Russian. The names of the kids I played with were Kalinowski, Napomaceno, Mollica, and Collins. To this day, if you ask someone from Waterbury where they live, they'll start by telling which end of town they're from. If they were Catholic, they also told you what parish they belonged to. Each end of town had two, if not three, parishes. These were not parishes or part of the city like in New Orleans. These were parishes set out and determined by the Catholic Church, and each had an accompanying school. There were at least eleven parishes in Waterbury, and they mirrored the ethnicity of the neighborhood.

In the South End, there was St. Anne's, the French Church with a gothic structure constructed of gray stone with beautiful soaring spires and wide marble steps. It would have blended into any French city. My father grew up in one of the twin, six-family blocks of houses directly across the street from St. Anne's. There he attended French Mass with his parents, his four sisters, and three brothers. He would tell me stories of how he and his brothers would jump across the rooftops from one building to the other. He was very athletic and muscular, a beautiful specimen of a man. He excelled at any sport he took up, including ice hockey, baseball, swimming, and diving. He was as physical as my mother was intellectual. Lucky for me, he made sure that his kids were given the chance to learn to play sports and enjoy the outdoors. My mother would rather chew nails than put on a pair of ice skates or jump in a lake. She grew up in the East End of town and belonged to Sacred Heart Church, the Irish church. Sacred Heart was solidly built of red brick with little ornamentation, more apropos to the Irish countryside. My mother lived right up the street from the church, and the fact that the two even met was a stretch.

Chapter 5

Family Fun at the Beach

W*e didn't have a car* until the mid-1940s when we owned a turquoise Kaiser Frazer. It was more like a boat than a car, both in color and size. Most women didn't drive then, so only my father drove it. In fact, my mother, who was never a very confident driver, didn't get her license until she was at least fifty years old. I can picture her in her Plymouth Horizon with the seat pushed all the way forward and a death grip on the steering wheel. She never had an accident, but we don't know how many she caused.

As children, we didn't get to ride in the car often. If we wanted to go anywhere, we walked, or when we got old enough, took the bus. Trips in the car were usually from home to Danbury or Bridgeport to visit relatives, or a special trip to "the beach" for a week every summer in August.

From the time I was about five until I was maybe ten or eleven, we would go to Fort Trumble Beach in Milford, Connecticut. When we were a street away, we not only could see the water but also smell the salt air. We'd scream out, "There it is! There it is!" We were so happy to have arrived. To us, packed in the car like sardines with no car seats or seat belts, it seemed like a long ride. My mother and the baby, Jerilyn, were in front with my dad, and the three of us, ages two to six, were in the back, fighting for the window side. All the paraphernalia a family of six needed for such a trip was packed around us as well as in the trunk, including a crib and a stroller.

The cottage that was our destination wasn't on the beach; it was one street away about midway down a sandy road. There was a very small front yard with patchy grass and three wooden steps going up to a screened-in porch where there were three or four rickety chairs. There was a small kitchen, a combined dining and living room with floors were covered in linoleum, and a treacherous, narrow staircase that wound up to three small upstairs bedrooms. The place was always hot. Air conditioning was nonexistent at the time as far as we knew.

When we got there on a Saturday afternoon, my parents' friends Armand and Bena Fisher who owned the cottage, would be there to give us the key. But what welcomed us was the aroma of spaghetti sauce and meatballs. The dinner was a bonus for us because my mother never made a meatball in her life. The only time we had spaghetti and meatballs for dinner that wasn't from a can was when my parents would take us for birthday dinners to The Grotto Restaurant on South Main Street, Waterbury.

In the back of the cottage, there was a fenced-in yard with a small canal running behind it. Ducks would come every day to eat whatever my mother let us throw in the water, usually stale bread.

The week at the beach was like an open house. It seemed there was always company. The most fun visitors were the Descoteaux family—my father's four sisters and three brothers and their respective husbands and wives. They didn't always come at the same time, but they always came. I'm not sure who was more eccentric, the

Riding high on Dad's shoulder

sisters or the brothers. They were so very close, so very different, and so much fun. They were an important part of our lives, and I only realize now how lucky we were to have them.

David and me at the cottage

The oldest was Aunt Clare, who was such a lady. I never saw her in anything other than a dress, nylon stockings (probably attached to a girdle), low heels, and pearls. She and Uncle Gene Doherty were in love from the day they met until the day he died. You could just feel it. I never heard either of them raise their voices to each other, or anyone else. They never had children. I can't say that was by choice because there weren't very many effective ways not to have children in those days other than abstinence at the right times.

My mother considered Uncle Gene a savior when it came to my brother, David. Uncle Gene was a Waterbury police sergeant who more than once saved David from big-time trouble and kept it small-time until my brother grew up and could take care of himself.

What I remember best about visiting Aunt Clare and Uncle Gene at their apartment was the covered china candy dish on the coffee table on the living room. It was always full of chocolates when we got there and empty when we left. My Aunt Clare ate chocolate every day and drank a Manhattan every night. I'm sure that's where I inherited my fancy for a nightly cocktail and a love of chocolate. Uncle Gene did not drink; I don't know the details, but my mother said that he had been driving drunk when he was young and killed someone. I'm sure that story is buried somewhere in a newspaper archive.

Then there was Uncle Jack Hill. Uncle Jack and Aunt Myrtle made up for the lack of issue for Aunt Clare and Uncle Gene. They had seventeen children in total, and none were twins. Understandably, they didn't visit us at the beach. I imagine they could barely manage to keep track of all of them. I remember visiting them in Bethel, Connecticut, where they lived in a two-bedroom house. We all played outside, and when it got dark, we went inside. After about an hour, there was a knock on the back door. It was one of the children who had been missed and left outside. I also remember three kids sleeping horizontally across the bed when they were little.

From what I remember, Uncle Jack was a handful as well. The aunts and uncles would occasionally come on a Saturday night to our Lounsbury Street apartment and play canasta around the dining room table. Food and at least a few rye and ginger ales were served. We would be in bed, but we could hear everything, especially the raucous laughter. I know the only way they got Uncle Jack out of the house was to "shuffle off to Buffalo" out the front door. Poor Aunt Myrtle.

It was the same at the beach. Aunt Marie, Uncle Ben, and Aunt Helen would come for the day bearing food, hot dogs, burgers, rolls, and the "go-withs." After a day on the beach, we'd go back and grill in the backyard. I can still remember the smell from the grill. Somehow at the beach, even the burgers and dogs had a distinctive aroma, richer and more mouthwatering. After dinner, the adults would sit around the table, play cards, and laugh. When they would break into song and loudly sing, "Take Me Out to the Ball Game," we kids knew they must've heard the ice-cream truck's bell and hoped we hadn't heard it too. The ice-cream truck came by every night, and most nights we got ice cream—and always when the aunts and uncles were there. When I asked my sister what she remembered most about my father's brothers and sisters, she said it was the laughter. They always had a laugh.

The highlight of the beach week was going to Savin Rock in West Haven on the Friday before we were going to leave. We could hear the music from the merry-go-round before the car was even parked, and we all shouted out what we wanted to do first. We'd walk up the midway with the throngs of people, stop to watch the cotton candy spin onto a paper cone and the caramel corn popping in the popper. I don't remember my mother ever saying we couldn't have something or do something, but I do remember her saying I had to hold my sister's hand. Holding my sister's or brother's hand kept me grounded, but the best part about being the big sister was that, when we reached the carousel ride, I got to ride the hobby horse that went up and down all by myself. My mother would sit with the little ones on benches shaped like lions and my father would stand by the horse and hold on to David. What was most fun about that ride was the challenge of trying to grab a ring out of this little chute as you flew by on your horse. If you got the gold ring, you got a free ride.

In the 1980s, my mother replicated this family experience at a cottage on the beach for her seven grandkids every year for two weeks from the time they were toddlers until they were teens. This is Kay Descoteaux, who didn't even like the beach, the sun, the wind blowing her coiffed hair, or the water. I don't think she ever put a bathing suit on while she was there. What she loved more than anything was watching these children enjoy themselves and one another, just as she had loved seeing me and my brother and sisters together. For her sake, we never let anything come between us. My father wasn't into us kids as much, but because he was a beach person, every day with him meant there would be swimming, fishing, and kite flying.

My mother didn't really care if my brother or sisters or I came with her grandkids to the beach. The kids preferred it when we didn't come because then no one had to eat what they didn't like or go to bed at any specific time. Plus Neenie (her grandchildren's special name for her) made sure that candy and ice cream were always available. Sometimes, my youngest sister and I would drop in for a day or two, but that was about all we could take of the seven kids together. There were occasional battles of wills, which my mother would referee. My sister Kath and her husband, Harry, did stay. Harry would commute to work in New Haven every day, an easy commute from Milford. (Harry is another story! A great guy, but one who thought a woman's place is somewhere, but not in a man's place. We had our minor confrontations. We kept them minor out of respect for each other.)

Kath and Harry both loved the shore, and their daughter Teresa, a toddler, was the youngest, so she needed watching more than the others. She had plenty of attention from the other kids, and all the kids got plenty of attention from Kath. Kath loved the kids, and they loved her. There were always games to play, and the kids were always included. When we were all there, we spent most evenings around the table playing some game. And laughing, of course.

It wasn't an exact replica of our beach days in the 1940s and 1950s, though. My mother didn't take the kids to Savin Rock, but instead to the arcade to play video games. What was the same was the open-house atmosphere. In the 1980s, the great aunts and uncles of the little ones would visit for the day, bearing hot dogs and burgers and all the fixings. They still looked the same. The "girls" were in striped shirts, pedal pushers, and white sneakers with turned-down socks, and the men wore T-shirts, khakis, and loafers. They were all probably in their seventies by this time and still as crazy as ever and as much fun.

Chapter 6

Grammar School

As a kid, *St. Francis Xavier* was our family parish. The church, school, church hall, rectory, and convent took up one whole block of the neighborhood. On the side street, there was a public school where the girls went for sewing and homemaking and the boys went for industrial arts and woodworking. (OMG, what century was that?) The beginning of my fifteen years of Catholic indoctrination began there, starting with the *Baltimore Catechism* being burned into my brain.

"Who made you?"

"God made me."

"Why did God make you?"

"To know, love, and serve Him in this world."

In 1946, when my mother started her career at Naugatuck Chemical, I started kindergarten with Sister Genevieve Marie. To me, she was at least seven feet tall, and I don't think she ever smiled. She clapped her hands to get your attention, and you stopped whatever you were doing immediately because if you didn't, you could end up in the cloakroom. Can you imagine? They put sassy or misbehaving kids in the cloakroom, a long closet running along one side of the classroom with sliding doors. And then, Sister would close the doors. Damn scary!

Sister Genevieve was the first of many nuns, at least twenty, who taught me. Whether they were Sisters of St. Joseph or the Congregation of Norte Dame, they all smelled the same and dressed the same: black robes, black veils with white coifs, and white wimples. I think many of them thought in black and white as well. If I were blindfolded and put in a room full of people with a few nuns in it, I could smell out the nuns. It's the kind of smell that wafts up when you're ironing a piece of linen with a steam iron—subtle and clean. I took piano lessons from Sister Genevieve in the convent, and the convent smelled the same way. It also was eerily quiet, like a tomb. I hardly dared to breathe.

Everyone walked to and from school twice a day. It was probably four short blocks for me. Parents could hook young kids up with older kids in the neighborhood to walk with, so they didn't need to worry. Not everyone had cars, so there wasn't any traffic. There weren't any drugs either, and there weren't as many creepy characters. Don't get me wrong—there were some creepy characters; they were just subtler. By the time I was in second grade, I had at least three or four friends to meet up with as I walked along.

I was a good student, never got into trouble, never caused trouble, and rarely got less than an A on my schoolwork. The only time I was in the cloakroom was to hang up my coat. I had just enough fear of the nuns to not stray from the path of righteousness but not so much that I was tongue-tied. I wasn't afraid to ask questions or raise my hand to answer them.

After school, just like every other kid in those days, I went into the house, changed my clothes (maybe!), and went right back out to the street, no matter what the weather was like. I can still remember how, during a hot summer, a torrent of rain hit the hot tar in the street and the smell was so fresh and clean—almost like a nun. I remember other days riding my new Columbia two-wheeler bike for the first time, which I'd received for Christmas, or wheeling the doll carriage with my new Betsy Wetsy doll inside. I'd also roller skate if I could find the skate key in my bedroom used to tighten them. Often I couldn't find two socks that matched, much less the skate key.

Growing up in a neighborhood like that, we were never allowed to say that we had nothing to do. Why bother? The answer would have been to go outside. All the neighborhood kids were outside, so there was always someone to do something with.

It was easy to establish close friendships with classmates who were also my neighbors because families didn't move from place to

Christmas was always special. The fireplace was fake!

place much then. There was no reason to. I can still remember the first and last name of every kid in my grade school class of twenty-seven. I made friends with everyone for my first four or five years of school. Then, when I was around eleven, I seemed to gravitate toward certain people. What makes you choose friends at that age? I wish I knew. I only know the friends I chose then were my friends for the next twenty years. Some are still my friends now, sixty years later. We never have to explain ourselves to one another, and we still laugh and cry at the same things.

I made five close girlfriends while in grammar school, and—there's no nice way to say this—we were a snobbish clique! "The Big Five," we called ourselves. We weren't cruel to anyone, but we weren't always nice either. We did everything with one another. Sometimes all five couldn't do everything because some had strict parents, but one or another was always available. I was always available! There was very little that I wanted to do that my mother wouldn't allow. I'm not sure if that was because I was sensible and serious or because she was just too busy to be concerned. I always asked my mother and not my father; he was more apt to say no.

My friend Jo, who had lost her mother when she was born, had no option but to ask her father. He would usually say no, especially if there were boys involved. When she tried to wheedle her way to get him to say yes, she'd say, "Nancy can do it!"

Of course, he'd say, "I don't care what Nancy can do. If Nancy jumped off a bridge, would you follow her?"

Usually, I would be standing right there when he said that, and I'm not sure how that made me feel. I don't think it was a good feeling. Why would I jump off a bridge?

Grammar school was *Happy Days* perfect, just like the 1974 television series about the fifties. At school, we did reading, writing, and arithmetic with a little history and geography as well as music, which was really just singing, and of course, religion. Yes, religion was tightly woven into our education. It was difficult to tell where one stopped and the other began. We'd say the Pledge of Allegiance

Dad, Mom, and family in their Easter best

every morning and recite the Lord's Prayer, starting with "Our Father who art in heaven." Every May, we sang the hymn "Oh Mary, We Crown Thee with Blossoms Today" as we marched outside in all our innocence. There would be a crowning of the statute of Mary, but I was never selected to do it myself. That was usually one of the girls whose father was an usher in the church or whose mother made fruitcakes for the nuns. My parents did neither of those things.

In second grade, we made our First Confession and First Holy Communion when we were seven years old, the age of reason. After that we had to go to church every Sunday or we would go straight to hell, dying with a mortal sin on our soul. When we were little, we went to church as a family. If my mother was home with a new baby, my father would take us, but we all went as a family at Easter and Christmas. By sixth grade, I went to Mass with my friends. By then, we all belonged to choir and would sing at the nine o'clock Mass on Sundays. I think the real reason all my friends joined choir was that after choir practice on Friday nights, we would walk a few blocks to John's, a local pizzeria, and split a small pizza. Maybe meet the boys too.

By seventh grade, it was all about cheerleading and boys for us. Cheerleading was a big deal and one of those "cliquey" things that excluded most and favored the lucky few. That's what we thought anyway. Cheerleading then was all about cheering at the boys' basketball and baseball games. There were no organized sports for the girls. May I repeat: no sports, no sports, no sports for girls—I can't say that often enough—just following the boys doing their sports. I'm angry today about how girls were excluded from having their own school teams then because I was well coordinated and strong, very capable of being competitive in team sports. But girls didn't think much about even the possibility of it back then. It was so outside the realm of 1950s reality.

There were as many beautiful public parks in the city as there were Catholic parishes. We could walk to all the parks. The architect of one of them, Fulton Park, was Frederick Law Olmsted, who designed Central Park in New York. Fulton Park had greenhouses where horticulturists grew the flowers and shrubs for all the parks in the city. Most of the parks had swimming pools, playgrounds and tennis courts complete with supervisors and lifeguards. When we weren't playing in the street, we would spend our summer days at the park, and I was expected to take my brother and at least one sister with me. We were so lucky none of us got hit by a car, drowned, or were lost. I was probably ten or eleven years old at the time, and my siblings were six and eight. It was a burden to me at the time, and now I think of the responsibility I was given at such a young age.

There were a few incidents, maybe more. Once my father dropped me, David, and Kathy off to go swimming at the beach at Scovill's Dam. He went across the street to work on the garden plots that Scovill's had offered to their employees. Left alone, we were fooling around and running through the outside shower when David pushed Kathy into the metal piping that went around it. She split her head open, and there was blood everywhere. In a panic, I ran to get a supervisor to find my dad so he could take her to the emergency room at the hospital. I didn't get blamed for that, but my brother did.

In our family, David got blamed for everything whether he did it or not, which was another point of contention between my parents. David was fearless, and often he did cause the problem, but my father was too quick to punish him and my mother too quick to defend him. If I was my father's favorite, David was my mother's.

In the winter, the baseball fields at the parks would be flooded for ice skating. We would skate every day when the ice was frozen, either after school or at night. By this time, the boys were chasing us on the ice, and we loved it. I didn't have to take the kids with me there because they still needed help with skating, and I would often meet my friends there at night. I would walk by myself through Mulcahy Lots to Washington Park—a dark, desolate shortcut through the woods with no houses around. I didn't think twice about it, but once when I was walking home, I thought I heard twigs crackling behind me. I literally ran home, flying over rocks and blueberry bushes until I got to my street where there were streetlights.

Occasionally a boy would ask if he could walk me home, and occasionally I said yes. I distinctly remember one time when this really nice kid, Don D., walked me home through the woods. He kept insisting on carrying my skates, and I kept on insisting I could do it myself. My mother had told me that independent streak started when I was two years old. When I think about it now, Don was probably too nice and didn't appeal to me. They say you marry your father, and my father was a bad boy when it came to women. Hence, the bad boys were always more appealing to me and still are, which is why I've been a single woman for the last twenty years! I did try marriage a couple of times, *try* being the operative word. More on that later in my story!

Chapter 7

The Monumental Move

In June 1955 there was, I felt, a cosmic shift in my life. The owners of the three-family house where we lived on the first floor decided they wanted to live there instead, so that meant we, as well as my Nana and Pop, had to move. My grandparents were both in their seventies now, and Pop was not feeling well. I'm not sure what drove my parents to decide to buy a house, but they found one large enough for all of us and one they could afford.

It was way across town . . . not only one bus ride from where we were but two. I was devastated. Luckily, I was able to graduate with my friends from grammar school before we moved. We would all be going to high school the next year anyway, but I never really adjusted to the new place. The move took us to Harvard Street in a place called Waterville; it was still part of the City of Waterbury, but to me, it was the boondocks.

The house was an okay house, kind of like the one in the book *House of the Seven Gables* but with only three gables. It was tall, narrow, and had three levels. It did fit all of us—but barely. There were three bedrooms: one large bedroom with an alcove along the front of the second floor where my two sisters and I slept, a master bedroom, and a very small bedroom. There was one bath.

My unassuming, self-deprecating mother was again the pillar, the person to the rescue, the core of the family. Pop was diagnosed with leukemia a few months after the move, and he and Nana ended up in the master bedroom until he passed away in December of that year. I have no idea where everyone slept during that time. I just know my mother gave up her bedroom, and evidently so did my father.

The summer of 1955 I took the bus from where we lived in Waterville, got off downtown at the exchange place, got a transfer, and took the Baldwin Street bus back to Washington Hill just about every day. Then I did it in reverse every night. In all, it probably took about an hour each way, depending on the connections. I didn't think twice about it. I just knew I wanted to be where my friends were. My mother evidently thought it was okay—or maybe she didn't realize it since I didn't tell her. She was in New York working, of course, and my father's shift was from three in the afternoon to eleven at night in Scovill's, and some days he golfed before work. So, I was pretty much my own master. No one seemed worried.

On the night of August 19, 1955, though, I never made it home. It had been raining buckets all day and into the night, but I still met my friends downtown. It was my birthday, and we were going to see Rosalind Russell who was appearing in person at the State Theater for the premier of her movie *The Girl Rush*. But she wasn't the only one who came to Waterbury that day. Hurricane Diane did, too, and flooded the Naugatuck River, washing away bridges and the railroad tracks over them, literally splitting the city in two. No one could get from one side of the river to the other that night. The flooding devastated the Naugatuck Valley landscape and washed away seventeen multiple family homes along the river from

Waterbury south to Ansonia and Derby. Some families were washed away, too, when they couldn't escape their homes in time. In total, fifty-five people were killed. That night, when I could finally get to a pay phone to call home, I learned there was no way my father could pick me up from our side of the city. But luckily, I was with friends from my old neighborhood whose parents could get to them, so I stayed with them that night. I didn't mind.

While I struggled to get used to living in Waterville, my younger brother and sisters adapted with much more ease to the new neighborhood and school. They were eight, ten, and twelve years old, and they didn't seem to break stride. Dave was the leader of their little pack, and Kath and Jerilyn were known as Dave Descoteaux's little sisters. They were very close to each other, had many friends in common at school, and David was very protective of them. I remember him teaching the girls how to bop to rock and roll music in the living room, but I didn't pay them much attention nor did they notice if I was there or not. I was very different from them.

I have to say here that Kath and Jer seemed to grow up painlessly and emotionally trauma-free. Kath was about as sweet a child as you could wish for, and she is now the sweetest adult. She was the most Irish-looking: blond, fair-skinned, blue-eyed, and petite. Just like my mother, she makes no waves. Jerilyn was the youngest and willful, maybe a little spoiled. She had no problem making waves and made her share with the Rat Pack Motorcycle Club—and literal waves living and traveling aboard a boat for fifteen years. She still carries a gun and challenges all norms. Kath and Jer were always best of friends despite their differences, and they were always close to David. He was their big brother and their defender. However, he also became very protective of me many years later when I was in a very threatening situation. I didn't exactly feel like an outsider in my family, but I wasn't part of David, Kathy, and Jer's little clique. My day-to-day life was very different from theirs, especially when I started high school and became active in a Catholic Youth Organization (CYO).

Every Catholic parish had a CYO specifically for the public high schoolers to continue their religious education, but the group was also open to any teen in the church parish. There was always a social with music and dancing after the religious instruction, so there was no way I wanted to join the CYO at St. Michael's, our new parish. Instead, I joined the one at St. Francis and continued to go back to the old neighborhood, even though it meant taking a bus on Monday nights back and forth that first year. That CYO was my savior! It had athletic teams, too, so there were baseball and basketball games to go to and parties to attend afterward. It was my only regular social interaction with guys, and after the first year, I was dating. That meant I would be offered a ride home, so there would be no more buses. I dated a couple of guys from the old neighborhood and the CYO for most of high school, so I always had a date for prom, but I never got invited to any other high school proms.

Chapter 8

High School

Four more years of Catholic inculcation at Waterbury Catholic High took me decades, well into my thirties, to get over. Why I chose Catholic High is beyond me. Of the "Big Five Friend Clique," four of us decided on Catholic High, and one, my best friend, Joyce, chose Crosby, the public high school. The two schools weren't that far apart geographically, maybe just two blocks, but my path and Joyce's up to that point had been in lockstep. Now her choice and mine were totally at opposite points on the spectrum. Her choice exposed her to new friends, different philosophies, religions, interscholastic competitive sports, and dating. My decision wasn't the best for developing a social life or practicing and learning from dating relationships. Today, it feels like that four-year period narrowed my perspectives and limited my opportunities, but I got a heck of an education.

Waterbury Catholic High was an all-girl school with 100 percent of its focus on education. We wore uniforms every day: blue jumpers, white blouses, and stockings. There was no makeup, no lipstick, no talking, no answering back. If you were smart, based on your IQ test results that nobody uses any more, you were assigned to classical college prep courses—unless you knew you wanted to be a secretary, and then you took commercial courses. It all seems so rigid now. I wish somebody had advised me to take a damn typing class! My life would be so much easier now. But no typing for me. Instead, every day I carried home a stack of books two feet high— literally not figuratively. These books were for my class work from English literature, Latin, French, algebra, geometry, trigonometry, biology, chemistry, organic chemistry, history—ancient, world, and American—and four years of religion. We had homework every night in every subject.

After school, my friends and I would walk with books in hand a few blocks downtown to the Handy Kitchen, a luncheonette where kids from all the high schools would convene before they took a bus home to different ends of town. The Handy Kitchen was a hangout like Arnold's Drive-In was on the *Happy Days* television show. It had a stainless-steel counter and stools covered in red leather, and about a dozen black booths across the room. If you got there before the crowd, you could grab a booth and hopefully George, the bald-headed, hairy-armed Greek owner with the white apron, wouldn't come over and throw you out if you weren't ordering any food. If he did, you'd order fries to go with your Coke. Naturally, there were boys there as well, so that was an attraction. If you were lucky, sometimes a guy would offer you a ride home while you were waiting for the bus.

I got through high school successfully. I tried to follow all the rules and did enough work to get As and Bs in my studies, but I never did as well in class as the infamous IQ tests indicated I could have. I did do well enough to be a "go-to" person for my friends when they needed help with schoolwork. I met new friends in high school—not lifelong friends, but good friends. One of these friends was Deb Denehy. That friendship was pivotal to my future, but I didn't know that until my senior year.

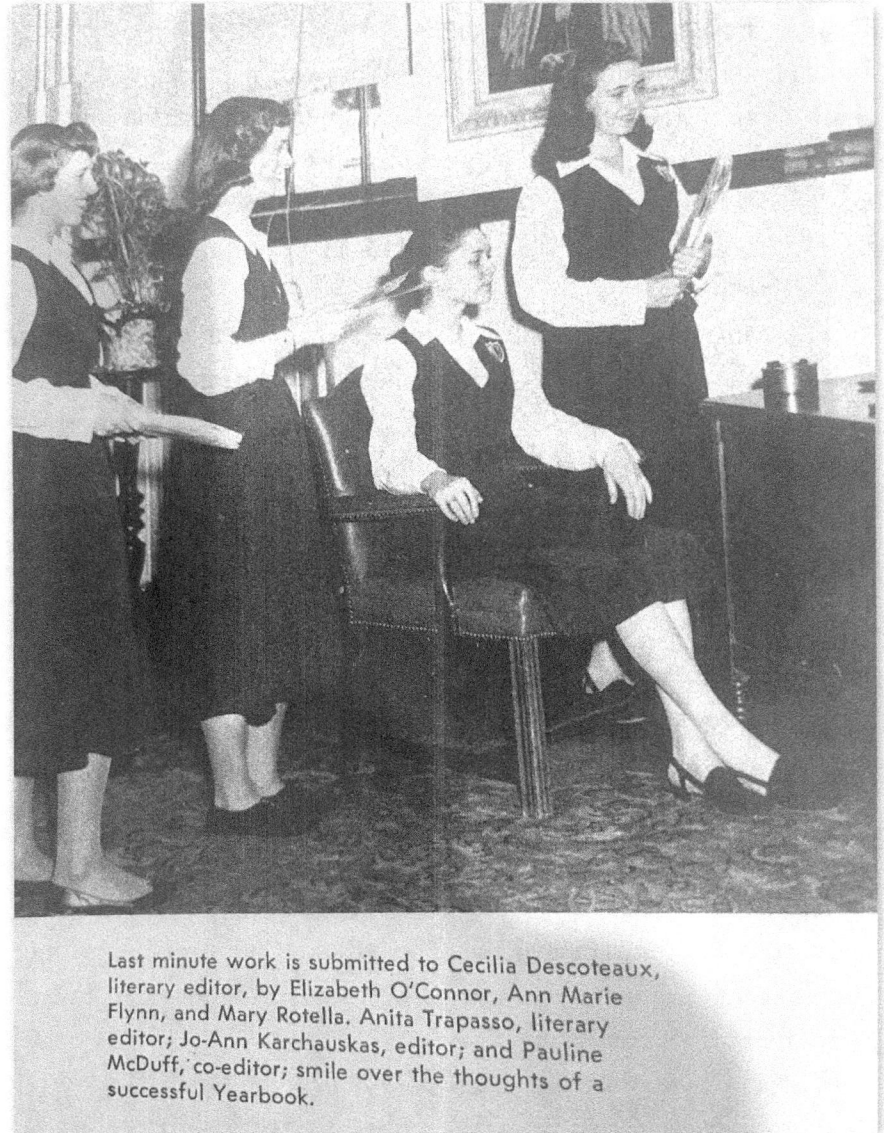

Last minute work is submitted to Cecilia Descoteaux, literary editor, by Elizabeth O'Connor, Ann Marie Flynn, and Mary Rotella. Anita Trapasso, literary editor; Jo-Ann Karchauskas, editor; and Pauline McDuff, co-editor; smile over the thoughts of a successful Yearbook.

At Waterbury Catholic High stylish clothes were not an option.

Who Was Joe?

In my neighborhood and in high school in the 1950s, there were two groups of kids. One was the "Hoods" and the other was the "Clickers." I was a Clicker. I wore saddle shoes, flared skirts, and sweater sets. I always dated "nice" guys—fellow Clickers, not Hoods. In my senior year, my new friend Deb, who was not a Clicker, introduced me indirectly to a guy who was a Hood. Hoods rode motorcycles or drove souped-up cars, wore black leather jackets, smoked, and drank. They wouldn't be caught dead on a baseball field. The Hood was Deb's boyfriend.

More importantly, he was her steady boyfriend through four years of high school, and whenever she talked about him, which wasn't often, she called him "Goopus." When I asked her why, she said because he had a funny face. She told me she was secretly engaged to him, but her parents did not approve. She was very smart, maybe a genius. She also had this weird gift: She could read, talk, and spell backward—not slowly but in normal conversation.

So, the first time I even knew of Joe Massicotte was as somebody else's boyfriend. The closest I came to him at the time was once when we were in Deb's car cruising by his house. She was so busy looking to see if he was home that she crashed her car into a huge oak tree in his front yard. There we sat in her white Pontiac convertible with the top down, the hood crushed, and steam escaping from the radiator, until a tow truck came and her father picked us up. I don't know how we got out of that situation, which is not unusual for me. I never seem to remember how I got out of trouble, but I can always remember how I got into it.

I met Joe Massicotte because of a fluke since our paths would have never crossed naturally. We didn't live worlds apart, but we led lives that were worlds apart. I sometimes wished we would have stayed worlds apart, but then I wouldn't have my children, Joe and Elise.

Joe was a nice guy, a carpenter by trade, three years older than me, but he was a Hood. He was a bad boy, and that's when I learned I was really attracted to bad boys. Though sullen and charismatic, bad boys aren't always Hoods. Some of the worst bad boys are preppies—think Brett Kavanaugh, current United States Supreme Court Justice despite allegations of sexual assault leveled against him during Congressional hearings on his nomination to the high court.

To this day, I still have that attraction to bad boys, which is probably why I'm single. I guess I can't trust my relationship decisions.

Joe was born and raised in Oakville, Connecticut, a small suburb of Waterbury, the youngest of four and the only boy. His parents lived through the Great Depression (1929–1939) in the States. They struggled, but they were resourceful French Canadians who were not afraid to work and could stretch a dollar. By the time Joe was born, Pepere, his father, had a good job as a painter at the offices of Chase Brass and Copper, one of the large manufacturing mills located in the Waterbury area at the time. Joe's dad worked long hours and was also a mean, explosive drunk. He once put a chair through the ceiling and flung a pie at his wife. When at home, he would sit in the dark in their den, smoking. But by the time I met Pepere, he was a church-going teetotaler who had given up drinking. He still wasn't around much for his son, but Joe had a doting mother and three older sisters—at least two older sisters—to spoil him, and they did. The third sister closest in age to him said he was always a brat, headstrong and trouble from the time he was twelve years old when he got so drunk that his mother thought he was going to die. He was also clever, smart, and industrious—not in a bookish way, but in a practical, creative way.

Joe went to an excellent technical school, one of the few still thriving in Waterbury, where he further developed his natural skills. There was no stigma in those days when it came to learning a trade. I can attest to the fact that he learned them all, but carpentry was his favorite. He could build, rebuild, and fix anything with or without plans or instructions. His parents bought him a car for his sixteenth birthday, a red Buick convertible. His mother said she looked out the window at the driveway the day after he got it and saw the engine parts scattered all over the ground. She thought his father was going to kill him. Joe had taken the car apart, but he put it back together the same day, all alone.

Joe graduated from high school and got a job at Arbor Homes in Woodbury as a carpenter. They were one of the first manufacturers of prefab homes that were ultimately delivered to every New England state. By the time I met him, Joe had been working there for three years and was loading and driving tractor trailers filled with the complete homes across the East Coast.

Although I knew of him through my girlfriend Deb, I finally met him in June of my senior year when Deb's father got transferred by his company to Cleveland, Ohio. After Deb left Connecticut, I didn't think about "Goopus" again until he called me one night out of the blue. We talked about Deb, and he said how much he missed her and that he was going to drive to Cleveland to see her. On that trip, Deb's parents probably prevailed or she came to her senses, and they broke up. He continued to call me, though, and we would talk. I was still in high school, and one day, I told him my friends and I were going to the beach for a day, and he offered to let me drive his car. Of course, he insisted that I would have to do a test drive, so we set a day. He picked me up, and we went for a short ride. It was far enough that he trusted my driving, and he lent me his car to go to the beach with my friends. I wasn't overly impressed with him, but I was attracted to him.

I had never known any guy like him. All the guys I had dated were my age, or maybe a year older. They grew up in my neighborhood, went to the same schools, belonged to CYO, played sports, went to confession and Communion, and maybe had a beer on rare occasions. They wore jackets with their school letters on them, not black leather jackets. They were just nice guys, but there was no mystery, no risks, and no excitement.

Joe was 6'1" tall with a slim but muscular build. It was easy to tell he did physical work and most of it outside. His face was long and narrow with a strong, square jaw and deep-set brown eyes. He had a head of thick, curly black hair that he tried to control with Brylcreem. He was clean-shaven, and his body reminded me of a young American Indian buck. His hands were large and strong. He would catch your eye on a beach, for sure.

Joe wasn't into clothes. He was aways more comfortable in work clothes or jeans and a T-shirt. I don't think he ever felt comfortable in a suit, although he had the physique and stature to wear one handsomely. All our married life, I bought his clothes for him. If we were going out, I laid them out for him.

When we met, he had his own money and car and a small space with a couch and a stereo in his father's cellar, where he listened to music from those popular at the time—Elvis Presley, the Everly Brothers, and Brenda Lee. He smoked Camel cigarettes and drank beer by the six-pack. I don't remember him ever missing a day of work. In fact, in all our years together, he never shirked work or responsibility. During the eighteen years we were married, we never had a plumber, electrician, carpenter, or contractor in our house. Joe did all the mechanical work on our cars, and when we decided to put an in-ground pool in, he did it himself with help from friends. There wasn't a tool Joe couldn't use, from a slide ruler to a sledgehammer and chain saw to a backhoe or bulldozer. He would climb up and top forty-foot trees and then climb down and have them fall exactly where he wanted. Then he would cut them to length and split them.

Joe didn't have many friends—just a couple of guys at work he would drink with and Larry, whose brother was married to his sister Alice. Larry and Joe were best buddies, accepting of each other on all levels. Larry ended up killing himself when his wife was going to leave him. That was a huge shock and a tragic loss for Joe.

Joe and I saw a lot of each other that summer of 1959. He was enamored of me, and I felt cared for and spoiled. He'd pick me up after work, and there would always be candy and cigarettes for me in the glove compartment. We'd go to Frankie's for hot dogs, Carvel for hot fudge sundaes, and when the first Golden Arches (McDonald's) went up, we enjoyed twenty-cent burgers. I met his family, and we spent much of our time with his sisters who had their own families and children. Their lives seemed idyllic to me back then. Their husbands worked, and they stayed home with the kids. His sisters were wonderful homemakers. They all sewed, were good cooks and bakers, and great housekeepers. They knitted and did macrame and decoupage. The Stepford Wives had nothing on them! I thought I wanted the same things.

I didn't realize that summer that I spent all my time with Joe and them on the weekends and not any with my family or friends. My mother reminded me of that when Joe wanted to get engaged and I accepted his ring against her wishes. She typed me a two-page letter, I'm sure with tears in her eyes. I still have the letter, and when I read it, I can have tears in my eyes.

Up until then, my mother knew I had never stepped out of line. I was the responsible one, the oldest of her four children, the good one. When Joe gave me a diamond the month before I was to start nursing school, everyone I loved was against it.

They said, "You're too young. He's not good enough for you. He won't want you to finish nursing school."

But I accepted the ring, and my mother was right. I wasn't the same girl and wouldn't be for the next eighteen years.

Part Two

The Struggle

Chapter 9

Nursing School

I don't know how I made it through three full years of nursing school. It wasn't like college with semester breaks and summer vacations. It meant being there seven days a week, every week, every month for three straight years with curfews of 10:00 p.m. during the week and 11:00 p.m. on weekends. If you did have a weekend off, which was rare, you were allowed to go home. Whoopee! It was called training for a good reason. In addition to classes, we were expected to rotate and work all shifts on all med/surg units and do eight-week rotations through specialties such as the operating room, delivery room, emergency room, and three months at the state psychiatric hospital, euphemistically called "Fairfield Hills" in Newtown. It was learning by doing, again and again and again. I think to this day I could insert a Foley catheter into a bladder with my eyes closed.

The nursing residence was a three-storied brick building behind the hospital on North Elm Street, almost directly across from Waterbury Catholic High School, the three-storied brick building where I went to high school. All the nursing students lived there and had all their classes there. It didn't look like a prison, but it felt like one at times. Yet strangely enough, sometimes it felt like a sanctuary. There were at least two hundred young women, ages eighteen to twenty-one years old, living there—freshman on one floor and juniors and seniors on the second and third floors. Of course, no men were allowed beyond the lobby, where two old crones sat to be sure that didn't happen. There was no smoking, no alcohol, no parties, and no exceptions. And no married women were allowed to attend. If you got pregnant, you were expelled. If you eloped and were found out, you were expelled, whether you had two years left or two weeks. I know because it happened to a senior while I was a freshman.

The first six months you were on "probation." Probation was like basic training in the Navy Seals. If it didn't kill you, you would get your nursing cap at a formal ceremony in the hospital chapel. Until then, you were at the bottom of the barrel. You were expected to go to 6:00 a.m. Mass (where they would check to see if your white shoes were polished), have breakfast in the cafeteria, and then attend classes for eight hours. The uniforms consisted of a pin-striped dress that fell to midcalf and a starched white apron and bib done in the hospital laundry. Looking back, we would not have looked out of place in Gilead, in *The Handmaid's Tale*.

During those six months, there were study hours from 7:00 to 9:00 p.m., and there were proctors on each floor to be sure you were studying. At 9:00 p.m., everyone would come out of their rooms, and there would be a stampede to the one pay phone on each floor and a fight over who would get there first to call their boyfriends. If one of us talked too long, the others would want to drag us out of the phone booth to end the call. To this day, I can tell you who talked too long. This included Bev Luddy and her soon-to-be husband

Timothy and Anne Brady and her soon-to-be husband Dave. My soon-to-be husband, Joe Massicotte, and I really didn't talk; we just listened to each other breathe because he was miserable and didn't want me to be there.

Those first months were a struggle. Joe fought me tooth and nail, arguing that I should quit because I was never going to work as a nurse. I was so lucky that despite the constant arguments and verbal haranguing, I successfully navigated the challenging academic load: anatomy and physiology, microbiology, medical/surgical nursing, pharmacology, organic chemistry, and nursing arts.

More than once when we would go out, he would refuse to take me back at curfew. I remember once opening the car door while the car was still moving. "If you loved me, you would quit" was his argument. And it almost worked.

My mother knew I was miserable. When I was home, which wasn't that often, all I did was sulk, do my laundry, and leave. I don't think she was surprised when right before capping, I told her I wanted to quit. I remember sitting in the living room with both my mother and father. My mother was pale, and her voice was shaky. She never liked confrontations and would yield on a point rather than fight. She must've felt she needed back up with my father. He didn't say much, just sat in the recliner looking shaken, but his presence told me how serious she was.

"Honey, I've never said no to you, but I'm saying it now," my distraught mother said. "I know you don't have a lot of respect for my working all these years, and I've let you make your own decisions." She had never spoken so sternly to me before. She always had the highest of expectations, and I think this was the first time I ever really crossed her. "You cannot quit training. You would never forgive me if I let you do this," she told me adamantly. I knew she meant it. I went back to the nurses' residence, sullen and crying, but compliant.

My mother was so upset about the idea of me quitting my nursing training that she wrote me a letter while I was still at school. She certainly was prescient about how my life might go with Joe in the future. Here's what she wrote:

January 18, 1960
Dear Honey,

Since things are turning out the way they are, I thought it might be well if I transcribed the notes I scribbled off to you the day after you got your ring. As you read it, you will see how right I was about some things.

When I called to say I was sorry about Sunday night, it wasn't that I had changed my mind or the way I felt about it. It was just that it seemed too bad that an event which should have been happy had to be done in such a way that the whole effect was spoiled.

I felt badly about it because I thought you would never do anything like that to me. I can't understand why you asked me about it, and [then] when I said no, went ahead with it anyhow.

Sometimes because of David, or once in a while Jerilyn, I feel like an awful failure as a mother. But then, I am so proud of you and the way you are, I think well, I can't be so bad after all because if I'm to be blamed for the wrongs, then I suppose I must take a little credit for the rights.

When I talked about your getting a diamond with different people, they all said you would get it anyway, and I was very quick to say no, not you, you would not do that to me, so you see it put me in a very awkward position.

You know I have nothing against Joe personally and anything I decide is for your happiness and your good. You have been going with him such a short time, and you know yourself there are certain things about him on which you have reservations. I had decided in my own mind that perhaps when you had been going with him a whole year and then still felt the same way, then I would say it was alright.

Since it seems he insisted on your having the ring, now I wonder what will happen if he insists on your not finishing your training. Different people have said you will never finish since you are so serious about him. I have always said very definitely you would finish, and I had no doubt about it, but if you go ahead now and get the ring in spite of what I said, then I suppose there is always a chance that Joe will insist on getting married and that will be the end of your training. I can hear you now saying you will definitely finish, but I wonder. I think that would be the final straw that would break my heart.

The ring itself doesn't upset me half so much as the idea behind it. After all, it is only a piece of metal and a stone. What worries me most of all is that you are so young and yet you are so serious about things. I am wondering if you found you had made a mistake, would you feel as though you had to stick to the bargain and make the best of it.

You probably don't realize it, but you have been an entirely different girl since you started going with him. In the first place, you're not the happy girl you used to be. Another thing, you seem to have divorced yourself completely from your own family. The family picnic was one indication. The fact that the only time we see you is when you come to change your clothes or pick up your laundry bothers me quite a deal. It is a very bad thing to spend all your time completely with his friends and his people. After all, your own family, and I don't just mean Daddy and me, have always been good to you over the years. They were the ones that brought you gifts on the different occasions in your life calling for them. They have always been interested in and proud of you, and you should not feel you do not have time for them.

Well, Honey, that is as far as I got in my original letter a few months ago. I am sure if you read it carefully, you would almost think I was psychic because things seem to be turning out just as I feared. I am not sending it now to make you feel badly but just to let you know that as much as you seem to disapprove of me sometimes, I am not stupid or talking through my hat when I try to advise you. After all, I was only seventeen when I started going with Daddy, and it wasn't easy for us to wait but we had to, and don't forget, it was four years for us and not two and a half. So when I say I know a little of how you are feeling, I am talking from experience and not because I think I know how it is.

Also, you might realize that circumstances were even a lot harder on Daddy and me. He wasn't allowed to come to the house, and I wasn't allowed the freedom you have. Perhaps that's where Mommy made her mistake, though sometimes I think you feel I make all the mistakes. Well, perhaps I'm the way I am because I didn't want to be like Nana. By the same token, you may be a much better mother because you will benefit from my mistakes.

Well, I won't say anymore. We will talk at home on Saturday or perhaps go out someplace where we won't be interrupted. Daddy is quite upset, especially since I broke down completely when I started to tell him about it. I tried not to, but I had such pain inside me I couldn't help it.

Well, this gives you a little idea of how serious it is. Think about it and pray about it, and I'll see you Saturday.

All my love,
Mommy

She must've called Sister St. Catherine, the rigid-as-stone administrator of the nursing program, because in a matter of days Sister called me into the medical library in the hospital. The first thing she asked was, "Are you pregnant?" My answer was no, but for the fates, it could have been yes. I don't remember what else she said, but she was evidently convincing. Another nun, Sister Mary Lorraine, the pharmacist at the hospital who had been a friend of my mother's in high school, also spoke to me. She didn't mince words: "Nancy, if you quit, you will break your mother's heart." I didn't quit.

Capping after probation was a big deal. Not everyone made it. It was a solemn occasion that took place in the hospital chapel. The chapel was small but very beautiful with stained glass windows, polished mahogany pews, marble floors, and an intricately crafted altar. There was always the lingering aroma of incense and a feeling of peace. The parents attended along with the nuns who taught us the basics those first six months. It was striking as we all marched to our pews in our blue-and-white uniforms and starched white aprons. Everyone was happy and relieved that we made it—except me. I was the saddest-looking probie walking down the aisle of the chapel to receive my cap. I never looked at my mother or father to see how proud they were. Thank God my mother saved me from myself. What should have been a joyous event was spoiled, as so many other events over the next three years.

Chapter 10

The Push and Pull

I *lived a double life for the duration of nursing school.* That's what I would have called it then; now I would call it "compartmentalization." It's something I was able to do throughout my nursing career and probably throughout my whole life. The rules were very restrictive in the dorm, and the classes were tough. Nursing is a discipline as well as an art, and the discipline requires strict adherence to policies and procedures, especially as a student. We really didn't practice the art until we had graduated and had some experience under our belt. I somehow not only adjusted to it but also thrived in the learning atmosphere and was able to focus when in class or working on the units. I didn't polish my shoes or attend Mass every day as was expected, and I had a plant in my room that I watered but was really used as an ashtray. I didn't always study either, but I really listened in class, so sometimes I didn't have to study that much.

I did well academically and clinically. In those days, the practicum was stressed much more than the theoretical. The students literally staffed the hospital day in and day out on all shifts. The expectations were very high, and criticism flowed freely and frequently. There was definitely a pecking order, and we were about as low as you could go, especially as freshmen and sophomores. Seniors got a tad more respect, and at the top of the pecking order were docs. They were treated like gods and most acted the part—and not in a kindly way.

Each clinical unit had a nursing station where the head nurse's desk was and patient charts were kept. There were a few small tables and chairs where nurses could sit to document their work, which was the only time the nurses really did sit down. The saying went that if you didn't document it, you didn't do it. There were no computers, no cell phones, no automatic pumps, no beeping monitors. This area was called the nurses' station, but if a doc walked into it, every nurse stood up, ready to give up *her* seat and get *him* whatever he needed. Believe me, the pronouns are correct because back then, every nurse was a woman and every doc was man. I know it sounds like the dark ages, and in many ways it was.

Hospitals had many more inpatient beds then. I think St. Mary's was a five-hundred-bed hospital, as was Waterbury Hospital. They were rival hospitals on opposites sides of town, one southeast and the other northwest, one Catholic and one nonsectarian. All operations, procedures, tests, and treatments were done in the hospital. There were no outpatient surgery centers or freestanding urgent care clinics. The only specialty areas in the hospitals were maternity and delivery, operating and recovery, and the emergency room. The other units were either medical or surgical, and they held the sickest of patients and the not-so-sick. We almost had no choice but to learn and become proficient or bear the wrath of the head nurse or the nun in charge of the unit.

Every unit had a charge nurse. Most of them were single women, and grouchy. Miss Behan, Miss Doherty, Miss Mathews, and Miss

Sullivan—I swear they never smiled except when the docs came on the unit, and they all had their favorite docs. A couple of them married their favorite docs. There were a couple, like Mrs. O'Leary and Mrs. Nani, who were almost human. Now that I think about it, most of the staff nurses who worked on the units during the day were single or newly married. The older nurses with families worked evenings, nights, or weekends so their husbands or sitters could take care of the kids. Most women were still not working in the early 1960s unless they were teachers or nurses. Female doctors, lawyers, and business professionals were few and far between. The women who worked had two jobs, home and away. If you wanted to work, you had to manage the house and kids as well and not complain or expect help. It was a man's world in every way.

As if the head nurse wasn't terrifying enough, every unit and department in the hospital had a nun overseeing it, with Mother Visitation, the CEO of the hospital, overseeing them. They were the Sisters of St. Joseph, and they were merciless. They would smile occasionally, but usually it was when they knew they caught you at something. I was quick enough and smart enough to stay under the radar. There was one nun, Sister Rose Eileen, who was well hated and terrified my classmates. I rather liked her because she was very sharp, insightful, and all business.

I remember her saying to me: "Miss Descoteaux, you may be able to fool some people, but you don't fool me. I know you're capable of much more than you are doing."

I had no response. I had heard that all through school. I didn't really push myself intellectually until I started my management career; then I operated on all cylinders. That career was not in my wildest imaginings when I graduated nursing school in June 1962.

I stayed engaged to Joe for those three years in spite of persistent resistance from him saying it didn't matter because I was never going to work anyway. The wedding plans were progressing that summer, and the date was set for September 8, the official day nursing school ended. Three years to the day! Gowns were selected, ordered, and

Nursing school graduation 1962

fitted. Photographers and DJs were booked. Showers and stags were attended. All the usual myriad details of registries were completed, invitations were sent, and the honeymoon was planned.

Graduation with two happy, relieved parents

Waffling

How did we get to this point of no return, marriage? Of course, I knew the answer to that, but it's still hard to admit.

Six months after meeting him, my mother said, "Honey, you're not the same girl you were. You're not as happy; you don't smile as much. You don't spend time with your family anymore. You're always with him and his family."

I ignored that observation then, but she was right. It was like belonging to a cult when your thinking becomes so skewed you don't realize you have sacrificed yourself, your authentic self, and you've become the shadow of another—either another person or a philosophical belief. The dawn did break eventually. I still have no clue what precipitated it, and I have no one to ask. It remains a mystery and a failure.

Three weeks before the wedding, sitting in his car in front of my house, I told Joe I didn't want to get married. We spent a lot of time in his car, a 1955 Oldsmobile that always made me feel safe and cared for. For three years, every time Joe picked me up, there were surprises in the glove compartment, like Hershey chocolate bars and cartons of Winston cigarettes. Now I was trying to escape from marrying him despite the fact that 150 invitations had been mailed and wedding gifts had been delivered to the house. What was I doing? I can't remember what immediately preceded that night to make me feel so brave. It had to be significant. He had made the three years of nursing school a living hell for me. And that night, sitting in his car, I tried to give him back the diamond, needing to get out of this hellhole I had gotten myself into.

"I won't take it!" he exploded at me.

Still, I put it in his hand and watched him throw it out the window onto the lawn. Somehow, I gathered the strength to get

The wedding day 1962

out of the car and go inside, not looking back. He peeled out of the driveway. I can't describe the relief I felt. Though I was sad for him, I knew it was the right thing for me. Thank goodness there were no cell phones or texting, so I only had to ignore his calls when I was home. Now I understand why today women "ghost" men to end a relationship.

Three days later, I was upstairs in my bedroom when my mother walked in.

"Honey," she said with concern in her voice, "Joe's downstairs. He looks so sad. Maybe you should talk to him."

Even this woman, who knew me best and probably realized what it took for me to end it, succumbed to his pleadings.

He was pathetic. "Please, let's try again. I'll be better."

He went on, "I love you. I can't live without you." That was all it took.

So, the wedding was on for September 8, 1962. Joe looked so handsome. We were both so young and innocent with happily-ever-after expectations.

Everyone smiled, drank, and danced. Off we went to Lake George with our white satin bag full of money, showered with rice in our 1960 red MG sportster convertible.

Chapter 11

The Good Years

*I*t all felt good—*maybe not quite right* all the time, but good—
and it continued to feel good for many years. The first two years
we spent in a thirty-foot house trailer that had been gutted by
fire and Joe had totally rebuilt. There was nothing he couldn't do
with his hands. I used to love to watch his hands when he worked,
especially doing carpentry. If you were marooned on a desert island
and had nothing but your wits to survive, you would want Joe as a
companion. You wouldn't have to worry. He would've built a boat,
which he basically did. We bought a small motorboat, a weathered
Penn Yan, a classic. He fiberglassed the boat one winter by himself
down in my parents' tiny basement. The house reeked of fiberglass
for months, but no one complained. My father and Joe got along
well, and my mother tolerated them both equally.

We spent many summer weekends on Connecticut lakes, including Candlewood Lake, Bantam Lake, Lake Waramaug, and Lake
Zoar, where we'd picnic and water-skied with friends. Waterskiing
is like bike riding. Once you get the hang of it, you don't forget it,

but there are some who never get the hang of it. Joe was an awesome skier on two skis or one. Thinking of it now and picturing him, I can still feel that physical attraction.

Our life was idyllic in so many ways. I was a new graduate RN working in the delivery room. Joe was working the three-to-eleven shift at Uniroyal, where my mother had gotten him a job. Sometimes after work at eleven, we'd get a bite to eat, and often, we'd play double solitaire until the wee hours of the morning, then sleep in until it was time to get ready to go to work. The biggest issue in our relationship up to that point was that I couldn't make a fried egg over light.

In 1964, we sold the trailer to my brother and sister-in-law when they got married, and we bought a small starter house with an acre of land in Prospect, a small suburb of Waterbury. It cost us $15,900 at the time. I remember we had to ask my Aunt Ciel to lend us five hundred dollars toward the deposit.

My Aunt Ciel and Joe had a love-hate relationship. When he insisted on giving me a diamond that she thought was very small, she made it perfectly clear to him and to me that she thought he was not good enough for me. Over the years, they more than tolerated each other but would still trade barbs in a somewhat friendly way. She did enjoy a cocktail, something they had in common.

There were times when their overindulgence in drinking led to uncomfortable situations between the two of them. The Mexican hat dance controversy was one of them. Aunt Ciel was the antithesis of my mother. My mother was serious, tolerant, humble, and a teetotaler. Aunt Ciel was self-centered, conceited, righteous, and a party girl at heart. She partied at family weddings, as we all did—all except her new husband, Stan. Stan was Aunt Ciel's boss, with whom she had an affair and eventually married when he left his wife for her. He was a wealthy businessman who owned Benrus

Watch Company in Waterbury. Aunt Ciel also loved money and all it could buy: expensive clothes, jewelry, and hats, all of which Stan bought for her. He liked to keep her happy. She had very expensive custom-made hats, but Joe also had a treasured hat: a big old black Stetson. He didn't wear it all the time, but he took it with him to fun events and wore it after he had a few drinks.

It was after my sister Jerilyn's wedding in 1968. Our family weddings never ended with the reception. Instead, we ended up at my parents' house where the whole drunken group of family and friends were gathered except the now-honeymooning bride and groom, Jer and Bruce. Aunt Ciel had had one too many and Stan had not had enough. Joe had left his hat unguarded on a chair, and Aunt Ciel thought it would be fun to toss it on the floor and dance around it.

We all bought in and started singing the Mexican hat dance, but when we got to the final loud chorus, Aunt Ciel, with her left hand on her hip and her right hand in the air, stomped on the hat. Joe Massicotte was *not* a happy camper. One of his favorite sayings was: "I don't get mad; I get even." I wasn't sure where this was going to go.

Everyone laughed, but everyone knew this was not the end of the story. Suddenly, Aunt Ciel's custom-made hat with all its feathers and flowers was thrown on the floor. It seemed that Joe had quietly gone out to Stan's BMW and "stole" the hat. It was easy to do; no one locked their cars in those days. When Joe threw the hat on the floor, Aunt Ciel laughed, but Stan definitely didn't think it was funny. We all gasped as Stan leapt out of his chair and grabbed the hat—after all, he had paid for it—and took it outside to lock it in his car. Stan was the guardian of the hats at all the family events in the future.

We stayed in the starter house bought with Aunt Ciel's help for eighteen years. The first ten years were really all about us as a couple.

It was a great little family house, but we turned it into the perfect party house. While our young married friends from nursing school were living in apartments, having kids, and struggling financially to "save for a house," we never had to. For nine years, we both worked with two salaries and no kids. I always thought I would have four kids, so I was disappointed without them, but Joe wasn't. He never said he didn't want them, but he never said he did either.

Joe and me, happier times 1968

Before kids, we did everything together. Everything! We went to the dump together, worked the same shift, slept late, partied on weekends, entertained prolifically, and loved every minute. At times, I would feel constrained because I knew what behavior would precipitate his wrath, and I avoided those. Instead, I did nothing without him, and he did nothing without me except stop at the bar every night after work. Every night. No exceptions.

Over the years, Joe built additions, remodeled rooms, and invested heart, mind, and body into that house and property. He was incredibly resourceful, talented, and strong. There wasn't a project too complicated or tedious for him. He singlehandedly built a brick fireplace, from the hearth to the flue and chimney, in the rec room, where he had installed a beautiful antique mahogany bar with a brass bar rail he had removed from an old barroom. To finish it off, he put in a beautiful in-ground pool on the lower level of the property, after clearing the area of towering trees with his chain saw. There was nothing this man couldn't do, and he did it all expertly.

Joe made some great friends at the Southern New England Telephone Company where he had gotten a job as a lineman, first climbing poles and then working on lines from the elevated bucket on a truck. Dom Gallo, Lou Smith, Ed Garvey were good friends as well as drinking buddies. I got to know their wives, and they would often call me at 6:00 p.m. to see if Joe was home. The answer was usually no, which meant they all stopped at the Pines, a local bar, for drinks after work and would come home a little sloshed. We had great parties with these friends, though I think that after the parties, the wives weren't talking to the husbands because they drank too much, stayed too late, and had to be driven home. These are also the friends Joe counted on when he was installing the pool or pouring a concrete wall, and these are the friends who called on him when they were doing anything and needed an expert.

Of course, the husbands of my dear friends from nursing, Anne and Bonnie, also knew who to call if anything broke. It wasn't call Saul; it was call Joe. If we had stayed married, there were many stories we would have reminisced about over the years with our children and friends.

Most had to do with the misadventures of Joe, like the time the six of us went to dinner at the Rocking Horse, a jumping restaurant in Hartford. Going out to dinner was what we did on a Saturday night, enjoying drinks, apps, salad, dinner, dessert, and after-dinner liqueurs. Everyone had a favorite liqueur: Joe's was Anisette, mine Amaretto. On this particular evening, we were seated at a large round table in the back room, which was dimly lit. These days I would've had to pull out my phone and use the flashlight to read the menu. From our table, there was a long oriental rug runner that went from the middle of the room to the restrooms with tables on either side.

Midway through dinner, after a few cocktails, Joe went to the men's restroom. When he came back, he said to no one in particular, but loud enough that we all heard it: "Someone is going to fall over that buckled-up rug runner."

I had all but forgotten the comment later until I was returning from the ladies' room, and lo and behold, there was Joe Massicotte writhing on the floor.

Oh, crap, I thought, *here we go. Joe took a pratfall.* Another embarrassing moment for me, but I knew his real goal was to pretend he was hurt in the fall and get out of paying for dinner that night. Everyone saw what happened, and of course there was a fuss. The manager of the restaurant came over to see if everyone was all right, and Joe made it clear to him that one of our friends with us that night was a newly minted lawyer. Needless to say, we didn't have to pay the bill, which was quite large.

Like it said in a popular song at the time, we thought those days would never end and the romance would last forever. Perhaps it would have if we had remained childless.

In the meantime, I was playing the role of a *Stepford Wife*, and our marriage looked perfect from the outside. I passed up career advancement opportunities, didn't attend the "No-Husband" Operating Room Christmas parties, drove us home when Joe was more drunk than I was, laid out his clothes on special occasions, canned tomatoes, grew roses and tuberous begonias, and worked with him on every project he undertook. I could drive a nail, lay shingles, use a level, drive a dump truck, and work a backhoe. I bought high-gluten flour in ten-pound bags and made my own bread and pizza dough. I can't say I wasn't happy. We were able to do pretty much whatever we wanted when we wanted.

When John Kennedy was shot in November 1963, we got a train to Penn Station in New York City and then took a train to Washington, DC, at 11:30 p.m. We visited the Capitol and walked by Kennedy's body lying in state in the rotunda with hundreds of other shocked and somber Americans. We then turned around and took the trains back home. Our friends thought we were crazy, but those are the crazy things you can do when there are just the two of you with no other responsibilities. It seemed that children were not in our future.

Birth control had never been a problem; I just never got pregnant. There's a saying that grass doesn't grow on well-trod ground. You can interpret that as you wish, but it's something I wished I had known before I got married. It would've saved me a lot of angst. I prayed not to get pregnant for three years in nursing and didn't. For the next seven years, I prayed to get pregnant and didn't, despite making novenas and saying the Mother's Prayer nightly. I went through a myriad of tests, and Joe did too. I was on and off birth control pills for a couple of years to try to get pregnant. Nothing was wrong with us, and nothing happened.

After five or six years, no kids started to feel good—like total freedom, or what seemed to me like total freedom in the 1960s. We were both working days now. I was working in the operating room, and as long as I was home before Joe, and the house was clean, laundry done, and food on the table, all was well. I started taking piano lessons after work and was still able to get home before he did. We had bought an old, nonfunctioning player piano that Joe totally rebuilt over one winter, key by key and bellows by bellows. When it was finished, he hooked it up to an old vacuum so we didn't even have to use the pedals to make it work. Who knew it functioned on vacuum and not pressure? Joe Massicotte figured it out. His creativity was amazing and endless.

We took wonderful vacations, usually road trips since Joe refused to fly, mainly in New England and Pennsylvania, always including extended family. A few times, we rented cabins on an island in Lake Winnipesaukee in New Hampshire. My parents and sisters (who weren't married yet) and Joe's sister Dorothy and her husband and two young daughters, Kathy and Karen, joined us. We'd tow the boat to the lake and ferry everyone from the mainland to the island in multiple trips. It was work, for sure, toting groceries, luggage, and kids. It was rugged but my horizons were narrow then, and I really didn't think beyond the moment. In the evenings after dinner, everyone would converge on our cottage and drink and play canasta or Penny Michigan until the wee hours, then head back to their cabins along a densely treed path. In the morning, they'd all come back to our cabin for breakfast.

One morning, I was up making coffee when my father walked in. I looked up, and his forehead and nose were completely scraped and bloodied.

"What the hell happened to you?" I asked him. His nose almost looked broken.

"I was attacked by a bear when I was walking through the woods last night."

By now, everyone was up to see what was going on. (You can imagine the kids!)

"Dad, a bear attacked you! Are you kidding? What did you do?"

"I ran to the cabin with him chasing me."

That was the chatter for the next few minutes until my mother came sauntering in and heard the to-do. She looked puzzled. "What's going on?" she asked.

"Did you see Daddy's face?"

"Yes, I saw it when he staggered into a tree on the way home last night instead of using the flashlight. He's lucky he didn't knock himself out."

There was no bear. But my father stuck to his story every time he told it.

There were many good times in those years. I gave up thinking about getting pregnant and decided that this life was not too bad. Even Joe's mother, Memere, stopped asking. I did feel somewhat sad when I'd see my friends with their children, but it wasn't over-whelming. Adoption was never an option. I didn't want to have kids just to have kids.

Then, *pow*! After seven years, in 1969 I was finally pregnant. Everyone was overjoyed for us, and Joe seemed proud and pleased. As with many initial pregnancies, though, it wasn't to be. About twelve weeks in, I started to bleed and was put on bed rest. Joe was totally attentive, setting the ironing board up as a bedside table to serve me meals. He wasn't a great communicator of his feelings, but the worry was evident on his face. Sadly, I had a miscarriage at three months, and I was devastated. Everyone—family, friends, Joe—treated me with kid gloves. I was fragile, weak, and weepy.

For months, my friends were so sensitive to my loss that they were careful what they shared about their kids. Within the year, I gave up hope and enjoyed the life we had. Then, miracle of miracles, two years later, in 1971, I got pregnant. The manager and staff of the operating room made sure I didn't get the long, grueling surgeries and always had help with the lifting and transferring anesthetized patients. I was nervous about losing the baby through the whole pregnancy, but this time I delivered a beautiful, healthy son. It was like the coming of the Messiah. I should've named him "Jesus," but we named him Joseph after his father and grandfather.

Life took on a new dimension, and I loved it. For years, we had accumulated the material stuff—house, cars, riding lawn mowers, wall-to-wall carpeting (covered up oak floors—that wouldn't happen today!) rooms of furniture and appliances. I didn't have to work, and I wasn't complaining. He was a fun baby, always smiling and happy. Of course, why wouldn't he be? There was always someone to pick him up, play with him, rock him, read to him, and spoil him. His godmother, my dearest friend, Doll, was a pediatric nurse at St. Mary's, so if he had the slightest cough or ailment, I could just call her for expert advice. She was always there for my son, even through college, replacing his bike at least twice when it was stolen and never chastising him for not locking it up.

Weekdays were my own if I was home when Joe came home, supper was on the table, and there was sex on demand. I was even able to work one day a week, but only because my sister-in-law Dorothy was willing to watch the baby. I'd get myself and the baby up and out of the house by 6:30 a.m., drop him off at her house, and head to the OR, and then pick him up at 4:00 p.m. I would never leave him with a sitter, and thankfully I didn't have to.

After the birth of my son, Joe, I didn't think I needed birth control. I thought one and done. Wrong again. Joe was eighteen months old when I had Elise, a beautiful little girl, in 1973. I felt blessed and thankful. Both Joe and Elise enhanced my life then and do so even more now.

Life was still pretty good. I loved being a mom, and I didn't mind being Betty-Home-Bake either after working full-time for almost ten years. The energy and focus I had expended at work were now centered on hearth and home. It had been easy with one, but with two toddlers, not so much. I remember grocery shopping with two carts, one for kids and the other for groceries. It never entered my mind to ask Joe, their father, for help with the kids or household stuff. We had an unspoken contract that the kids and every responsibility connected to them were mine to manage. There were many unspoken contracts between men and women in the 1960s and even the 1970s about roles and responsibilities. There were not many men—in fact, I knew of none in those days—who crossed over roles and shared childcare and/or housekeeping. Most women didn't expect it, and neither did I.

The Unraveling

One snowy day in February 1975, the unwritten contract I had virtually signed on to was verbalized.

It had been a brutal week weather-wise, with snow and more snow, nowhere to go, and no way to get there anyway. With two kids, work was no longer an option. Joe wouldn't allow a sitter in the house, of course, but I didn't want to work either. It was a battle I chose not to fight. If I had, I'm sure divorce or worse would've come sooner. I was at my wit's end with the isolation though. I knew I couldn't expect relief when Joe got home from work since he hadn't changed a diaper in the last two years or stayed alone with the kids. First, he didn't want to, and second, I didn't trust him to. The kids were too young to know the rules for staying under the radar. Not that he would ever in any way abuse them, but his thoughts on discipline were very different from mine.

On this dark, dreary day, when he walked through the door after the usual bar stop, the kitchen had been turned into a train of kitchen chairs. A cardboard box was the depot, and every pot and pan I owned was on the floor. I didn't care. It kept Joe and Elise busy for a while, but when Joe yelled out, "What the hell?", I burst into tears and said, sobbing, "I can't do this. I need a break."

Joe had frequently been gruff, and his responses were hurtful to me. His mother used to tell me, "Don't pay attention. He doesn't mean it."

She was used to it, but this time his growled response took me aback. "You wanted them; you had them," he said. "Now you can take care of them."

Suddenly the words were no longer unspoken, and their meaning was crystal-clear to me. I just looked at him and thought, *As soon as these kids can brush their own teeth, I'm out of here. I'm out of this marriage.*

That night, as I disassembled the "train" and got supper on the table, was the first time I thought about leaving Joe. That thought stayed buried for four more years, and it didn't bubble up until there was no other option.

I'm sure it would appear to an outsider that what seemed like a good marriage between Joe and me suddenly went bad for no reason. At times, it almost seemed that way to me when I was in the middle of the turmoil. But things really did go sour when I was no longer content to be Betty-Home-Bake, the kids could now brush their own teeth, and they were in school all day. It didn't take all day or a lot of gray matter to run a household.

I had no idea what to do with myself, now shades of my mother. I had crocheted enough afghans, spreads, and hand puppets to have my own craft fair. I had taught myself to sew and make draperies, dresses, and dog beds. I made Beef Wellington, Lobster Newburg, and Baked Alaska for more dinner parties than I could count. I hung the sheets out to dry, even in the winter, and I mowed the lawn when I got really bored. Again, it was picture-perfect from the outside looking in.

I was dying, but not physically. I felt like my brain was shriveling up. I tried, really tried, to talk with Joe about how I felt. About what I needed.

"Play cards with me; play Scrabble with me. Talk to me. I need more."

His response: "I don't know why women don't just want to stay home anymore." Then he'd add, "My mother did it. Why can't you? I am who I am. I can't change."

I felt like I was speaking Latin to a man who only understood French. Whatever I said I wanted or needed always seemed to get turned around, making me feel selfish and self-centered. Finally, Joe's solution was to say to me one day: "Do what you want during the day. Leave me alone."

I thought, *Okay, that might work.*

So, I took up tennis—and I mean, I really took up tennis. I met a young woman at the local park, Kathy, who is still my friend today, but now we golf together. At the time, we took our kids to the park, and we were both looking for an outlet. Tennis was it.

Eventually, Kathy went back to college while her kids were still little and got her degree in teaching. It didn't thrill her husband either, but she seemed to know how to fight for herself and stay married, a skill I never learned. Kathy and I began playing tennis together almost every day, weather permitting, and we played tennis year-round for the next thirty years. I played indoors in the winter with another group of "kept" women. They were married to doctors, lawyers, engineers, etc. They spent their time at the "Club" and would never have to worry or work for the rest of their lives. In my case, I had found an outlet for my frustrations doing something I was good at, and because I've never done anything halfheartedly, I was invited to play at the country club and in citywide tournaments. I only played when Joe was occupied working or otherwise busy. I thought it'd be okay.

It wasn't. Soon he started asking where I'd been all day, who I'd been with, and he made it clear he hated when I played tennis with "those rich bitches," as he called them.

It got to the point that my six-year-old daughter asked me, "Is Daddy gonna let you play tennis?" I thought, *Where the hell did that come from?*

I'm sure there's a name for my naïve thinking—probably in that book *Women Who Love Too Much*, but I seriously thought after years and years of faithfulness and compliance, he would learn to trust me and let go a little. I knew he loved me, and I loved him. He wasn't the boy next door, but he was handsome, charismatic, and mysterious. Unfortunately, what I thought was mysterious was really insecurity and chronic depression, so there was no loosening of any of the constraints I felt. Instead, it got worse with time, especially as Joe moved into his early forties which is midlife crisis territory. He then pulled the reins even tighter and tighter on me, and I was beginning to buck them.

Despite these ever-growing constraints, I enrolled in a creative writing course at the local community college. I thought it was a good place to start since I knew that at some point, I would need to get a bachelor's degree in addition to my RN. The course was during the day, so it didn't impact Joe's time. It was a great outlet for me, and it may have saved my sanity. That class started me keeping a journal, and I wrote in it every day for the two years that preceeded the end of my marriage. The class itself was stimulating and made me realize how much I enjoyed writing. It was something I couldn't talk about with Joe because when I did, he accused me of being in love with the professor. I could only look at him in disbelief.

He became more and more sullen and angry. He had always looked angry except when he smiled or laughed. He did have a million-dollar smile, but it was as rare as having a million dollars. Black curly hair, dark brown eyes, chiseled features—a romance novel cad look that almost always means trouble. As he withdrew even more and communicated less, I did the same. I did what I wanted when he worked and did what he wanted me to do on evenings and weekends.

All conversation became practical.

"What do you want for dinner?"

"Oh, by the way I'm working overtime tonight."

"Where are the kids?"

I started working one 3:00–11:00 p.m. shift a week in a nearby skilled nursing facility. I'm not sure how it came to be, but in my journal, I wrote, "Joe allowed me to work one evening a week as long as no weekends were required." I found a sweet young girl in the neighborhood, Florence, to come and stay with the kids from the time I left until he got home. I'd leave supper prepared and everything set out for the kids' bedtime.

By 1977 through 1979, I was just going through the motions. I started writing letters to Joe, which I still have, about how I really felt, but I didn't share any of them with him. All honest communication between us had stopped. There never was much conversation, so to all outward appearances, all was well in our marriage.

Toward the end of 1979, the situation intensified. He was drinking more and had started smoking marijuana. This led to episodes of him staying in bed for days at a time, crying.

"I know I have everything and should feel happy, but I don't," he'd wail. "No one can help me. It's not worth it."

By then, I was seeing a marriage counselor, and Joe came to counseling with me a few times. But when I asked him again, he'd repeat, "No one can help me."

I ended up continuing alone.

Chapter 12

Counseling for One

I can't remember who recommended Bob Raymond to me. Whoever it was said that he wasn't a crazy psychiatrist, but a psychiatric social worker. Bob worked at Waterbury Hospital but had a private practice that he conducted in a small waiting room and office in the front rooms of his home in a residential section of Naugatuck. The waiting room was always too hot but otherwise comfortable and calming. I never waited with anyone else and never saw anyone come out, which seemed strange to me until I learned there was a separate exit on the side so no one ever saw anyone come out.

Bob was also comfortable and calming. He was a little stocky, with thinning grayish hair, a peaches-and-cream complexion that would have been eye-catching on a woman, and a more-than-distinguished nose. He dressed like Mister Rogers: comfy shoes, slacks, a shirt, and a boring, beige cardigan sweater buttoned up all the way up. He spoke like Mister Rogers, too: softly, slowly, and thoughtfully. If Joe Massicotte had an antithesis, it would've been Bob Raymond.

I went by myself originally because I didn't know what to do. I couldn't see myself staying in the situation, but I couldn't see myself getting out either, so I had no vision of where I was heading. I told Bob my story. He asked questions. We talked about my mother and father—my mother's career and my father's cheating. I told him I couldn't understand why my mother didn't take us and leave him. She made as much, if not more, money than my father, so it wasn't financial. They hardly spoke to each other. Bob told me that everyone was not like me, able to decide to take action and then do it, even if it was the right thing to do. I didn't think about myself in that way back then. Now I do.

After weeks of going alone to see Bob, it came to the point that if we were going to work on our relationship, Joe and I had to do this as a couple. Over the past few months, sex had become a point of contention since it was the last thing I wanted to do and the only thing he wanted to do. I wanted to communicate verbally, not physically, but Joe felt having sex would solve everything. When I shared this with Bob, he said it wasn't the solution and wouldn't help to rebuild our relationship. Instead, Bob suggested that we should start from scratch in our relationship—what attracted us to each other, what we liked about each other, and so on. That sounded like a good approach to me.

I wish I could say I felt relieved and hopeful when Joe finally agreed to come with me to Bob's office, but I was too anxious. Driving there, Joe's face was frozen in a scary frown, ready for battle. The car felt like a vacuum had sucked all the air out of it. Not a word was spoken between us on the way there or in the waiting room, which was literally stifling that day. When Bob opened the door and called us in, my mind was numb. Bob started the session out painlessly. Joe shared how he saw things. For example, he told Bob that he couldn't understand why, all of a sudden, I wanted to live my own life. He had done everything I wanted. I didn't have to work. I only had to stay home and take care of the house and kids. I had everything.

I didn't say a word. I didn't have to.

Bob introduced the idea of how we would have to start from scratch, almost like we were dating, by saying, "Wouldn't it be worth it to build a new relationship? You'd have to start from the beginning with no demands on each other, no criticism, and only doing what you want for each other."

I knew what Joe's answer to this suggestion would be. Immediately, Joe asked the question I was waiting for.

"What am I supposed to do about getting laid?"

Patiently, Bob replied, "While you're working on rebuilding your relationship, you should abstain until you are mutually ready—a month perhaps."

With that Joe leapt out of his chair and screamed, "Are you crazy? That's not going to happen. I'll find sex somewhere else. I knew I shouldn't have come here."

Out he stormed through the door he came in—so much for the side entrance.

Bob and I sat staring at each other until I took a breath and he spoke.

"Nancy, you have been unable to assert yourself in your marriage. You and Joe have no relationship at this point. You cannot make him happy. Only he can do that."

Then he added, "Drinking isn't the cause of Joe's depression. It's the result."

I continued counseling with Bob, and it helped me cope because the more centered I became, the more crazed Joe became. It seems we both turned inward. I was silent, and he shut down completely. It felt like a pressure cooker was about to blow in our house . . . and one day it did.

Out of the Mouths

Things weren't good, but there were no screaming matches, no raging arguments—just an air of tension. It was the kind of tension that develops when there is so much to say and no way to say it. Certainly, neither of us mentioned the word *divorce*. It was still a dirty word, although surprisingly, the divorce rate in the late 1970s was the highest ever at 5.3 people per thousand.

Then, in 1980, I realized that the tension in the air was affecting more than Joe and me. By then, our son Joseph was eight-and-a half years old, and Elise was seven. Fortunately, we were blessed with two healthy, bright children who caused no trouble at home or in school. In fact, at my teachers' conferences that year, Joseph's third-grade teacher, Miss Orintas, told me that although he might be smarter than she, she was still the teacher, so maybe he did cause a little trouble. At Elise's conference, I learned she was a catalyst in school and a leader. This was my quiet one.

I thought the kids were unaware of what was going on between Joe and me. Their day-to-day life hadn't changed. Daddy went to work; Mommy stayed home and took care of them. There may have been cold, unexplained silences between us and hard, stony looks, but I thought they all went over the kids' heads. How blind I was!

One day, I was in the car with the kids, probably going to visit my mother or my sister, who were my major emotional supports. I drove past a quaint little church just down the street from our house and noticed a wedding was about to start. The bride was standing in the open door of the church, looking so lovely so I turned the car around and went back so the kids could see her. That was how the conversation began.

Elise asked, "Mommy, how many times were you married before you married Daddy?"

I told her I was never married before, only once, and would probably never marry again.

"How about Daddy? Was he ever married before?"

"Nope, just to me," I responded.

Then Joseph asked, "Mommy, just say you and Daddy got a divorce. What would happen to Elise and me?"

What the heck! It took me a couple of seconds to respond.

"Well, I think you and Elise would probably stay with me."

Elise chimed in. "I could stay with you, and Joseph could go with Daddy."

Joseph responded, "Yeah, I can make scrambled eggs, and Daddy can make an omelet. I guess we'd be all right, even though I don't like omelets. We'd have the car and the truck, and you'd just have a car."

Of course, Elise was not going to be outdone by a truck, so she added, "That's all we need."

"Well, I think you would both stay with me," I suggested.

"Yay!" Joseph said. "Mothers are more natural with kids. It would be okay if the Trumfios (our next-door neighbor) moved. Then Daddy could buy that house and live next door. We could still kiss him hello and goodbye."

Then I added, "What if I left, and you both stayed with Daddy in our house?"

"I don't think Daddy could handle us both, the way we fight."

That was it. They dropped the subject as quickly as they brought it up. They didn't seem overly concerned. I wish I'd felt the same.

I was "beside myself." I had never thought of that phrase in concrete terms. I felt literally beside myself. I moved through my day as usual, but I was on automatic pilot. Anyone watching me would see nothing untoward, but I was watching myself as well, from the outside. My mind was so detached from what I was actually doing; I was in a different sphere. It was frightening and at times totally uncontrollable. I would do things like back up the car without looking behind me. That was just a minor fender bender, but another time I left a lit cigarette in the car ashtray and caused the car to catch on fire. It was a total loss. I never told anyone what really happened. I just said the engine started to smoke and flames leapt from under the hood.

I don't think that state of mind serves any purpose, but I do know it can't go on indefinitely. I think it places you too close to that line that separates mental health from mental illness, reality from delusion.

The Brutal Truth

One night in May, I came home from work at 11:00 p.m., and Joe was waiting for me.

"I feel better. Alice came over tonight and we talked." He didn't say what they talked about, but I felt relieved that at least he was talking to somebody. We had spent many evenings with his sister Alice and her family, especially before we had our own family. We were very close. He did seem better . . . until I got into bed.

"It's gonna be the same sleepless night."

"What's wrong?"

"If I ever get through this," he said, "I'll never depend on you for support again."

"Haven't I supported you for the past seventeen years?"

"Support's not the right word. I don't know what the right word is. You destroyed me, ruined me. Or maybe I did it myself. I need a girlfriend, and when I find one, it won't just be for sex. The only reason I was faithful to you for the past seventeen years is that I was afraid I couldn't control myself and keep from getting involved."

I had thought he couldn't hurt me anymore. I was wrong. He could, and he did. How stupid I was to think that he loved me. It's no wonder we didn't communicate well with each other over the years—we were each living in our own worlds neither of which was real.

I rolled over, too stunned to respond.

A couple of days later, we took the kids to a roller-skating party sponsored by his company. Joe seemed strangely happy, a sharp contrast to the past few months. I actually saw him smile at someone, and it wasn't me. I skated with the kids, and he socialized a bit with coworkers.

When we were getting ready to leave, he said, "Do you mind if I go out tonight?"

He had never asked permission before. When we got home, he grabbed a six-pack of beer and left. I knew that something was off—a gut feeling.

He got home at 3:30 a.m. I never asked any questions that day. I didn't have to. I was sick to my stomach, sure he'd begun the search for the girlfriend he thought would solve his problems. If he thought being free of me would solve his problems, then he was taking the right path.

Later that day, I finally asked, "Where did you go?"

"Just out."

"Who were you with?"

"A friend."

He wouldn't deny or confirm that he was with another woman. I knew, and he knew I knew. We both cried in each other's arms that night, knowing that what had happened was a breaking point.

He said, "I'm not going into the pits of despair again." We made love that night. I don't know if we were consoling each other or trying to reach each other in the only way we had left.

We went to the counselor that Friday night, and when we got home, it started.

"I'm not going back. The counselor just wants to talk to you anyway. It won't bring the love back between us."

"What are we going to do about us?"

"I'm too dependent on you. It's not good. We should live more separate lives. I want to go out alone more. You shouldn't care what I do."

"What in hell are you talking about?"

With tears rolling down his face, he went on, "I don't know why I'm crying. I'm not depressed."

I couldn't stand to see him crying. It broke my heart. It was easier when he was angry and mean, lashing out at me. I didn't want him to feel alone, but it made me so vulnerable. It was easier when I isolated myself from him. I didn't want to lose him, but I couldn't lose myself.

"I cannot share you with another woman; I'll tell you that right now. I can't take the stress of this much longer."

'I don't know why you're so upset. You're the one who destroyed me and caused my depression. Now I've solved that. You were my life, but like a child breaking away from his mother, I have to break away from you."

"I'm not taking responsibility for your depression. I didn't ask you to make me the center of your life. You wanted to possess me—at least my body. You didn't care about me, about my thoughts, my feelings."

Then I went on. "The counselor told me I shouldn't expect you to change because you can't. I couldn't accept that because I thought you didn't want to change. The counselor said that's my problem."

This caused Joe to chuckle. "Maybe you need the shrink more than me since he's finding so much negative about you."

We spent the rest of the day avoiding any serious conversation. It was calm and uneventful, but nothing was resolved. Whatever was left of our relationship was on the brink of collapse.

The Roller Coaster Goes Off the Track

It was May 1980. Nothing was resolved, but sometimes it all seemed normal. Until it wasn't. Every day was an extreme; futility, then hope; terror, then tenderness; debilitating sadness, then remorse.

One night after the kids were in bed, I asked him, "Are you going out tonight?" He had started going out at night routinely, and I didn't care. At least I said I didn't care.

"No, I'm not," he replied.

"Then I'm going to run to Mother's for a little while."

He went bonkers and started yelling and screaming at me. "If you're going to start going out, that's it. I'm done. It's over. That's the last straw."

That was the last straw for me.

"I'm going to my mother's, and you tell me you're going out with broads. You don't see the difference. That's it. You have to leave. I can't take this craziness any longer."

"Never! Not without a court order!"

Then he proceeded to get drunk and later told me, "Go the f**# wherever you want."

He finally went to bed and passed out. His first words at 6:00 a.m. while we were still in bed were, "Okay, if you want me to, I'll leave."

I was relieved and agreed with him, saying, "Joe, if you stay here, something bad is going to happen. I'm afraid you are going to hurt me, yourself, or the kids. We can't live together right now. You've got to get help."

No response. He got up, got dressed, and left.

He came back around noon and started drinking—first beer, then vodka. I was getting more and more anxious, though I tried to appear normal. Thank God it was a beautiful spring day, and the kids were playing outside where I could see them. And then he started.

"You can bet I'm not gonna be leaving on my own. You can't throw me out of my own house."

I said nothing. I was too frightened. I tried to stay out of his way the rest of the day. After dinner, he said he was going to take the kids to the carnival. I had forgotten the carnival was in town. He had already told the kids, and I didn't want to make a scene with them, so I said fine.

The kids went out the door, and he left, but not before he whispered in my ear: "I feel like punching your face in."

I knew I couldn't take this much longer. One minute he said he wanted a divorce, then in the next one, he'd say he'd contest a divorce and make it ugly. I knew how ugly he could get.

That night after I put the kids to bed, Joe was back to suicide.

"I'm just gonna kill myself, and when I'm laid out, people will say, 'Look what she did to him.'"

I finally realized I needed to do something. By now, it had been at least eighteen months of serious outbreaks and threats. I wasn't in a panic, but I also didn't know if I had a false sense of security thinking he wouldn't really hurt me. That week I consulted an attorney. When I told Joe I had done so, he was shocked, but he didn't explode in anger. That surprised me, but then he told me that he hadn't stopped at the bar and he was going to stop drinking.

And then, the next day he told me to serve him with the papers and get it over with.

At that moment, I knew we were no longer "we"—each of us was breaking away, but we weren't quite there, and I wasn't ready to serve him with divorce papers. Within the next few days, he also sought legal advice and informed me that his attorney said I couldn't throw him out unless he harmed me physically, that the threat of harm is not enough. He still wasn't drinking, so the threatening had stopped. Surprisingly, he decided to see a psychiatrist, someone his attorney recommended. Joe asked me, "Is it worth one last shot?"

"I really don't know—that's up to you," I replied.

It was true. I really didn't know. I knew I couldn't live my life the way he wanted me to, and I couldn't see him changing. In his mind, my going back to school to get my BSN or even going back to work was rebelling against him. I wasn't sure a psychiatrist could change his mind on that.

True, Joe hadn't had a drink in three weeks, and he was continuing to see the doctor. He told the doctor the reason he was depressed was that I didn't love him anymore and our marriage had broken down. He also told me he made an appointment for us to go to see that same doctor for marriage counseling, but I told him there was no way I was switching counselors at this point.

Instead, I told him, "If the doctor wants to see me alone for your benefit, I will do that."

"Then I'm not going back either," he shot back at me. "The only reason I went in the first place was to save our marriage. I don't need any help."

I think he was furious at me for wanting to continue to see our original counselor, Bob Raymond. However, I did make an appointment to see his psychiatrist, but alone.

I went to see Joe's psychiatrist, even though I felt I was being manipulated by this doctor. I was so uncomfortable sitting across from him in his office. I felt like I was on trial. He was under the impression that I would come with Joe to see him. He said that I had the upper hand because I had better social skills. He told me

Joe had underlying problems needing attention that went beyond the marriage. He was not happy when I said I wouldn't be coming with him. He asked what I was doing to help Joe.

The doctor didn't like my response.

"I've been helping him for eighteen years, and it got me nowhere. I'm done."

I walked out of that doctor's office and breathed a sigh of relief. I thought to myself, *I'm changing my script. I'm going to follow my own path. Do the things I want to do and be the person I want to be.*

Chapter 13

The Point of No Return

For most of May and June I would stay up until Joe passed out and then go to bed. His depression and paranoia were worsening in spite of the meds he now was taking. Up until this point, I wasn't afraid he would hurt me—though he had put his fist through the wall, causing my nine-year-old son to ask if The Incredible Hulk had been here. That was the first time I had ever seen my husband become physically violent.

Joe refused to come anywhere with me and the kids, even to see our dear friends for the Fourth of July. It was something we'd done for years, and he must have felt so alone. My heart ached for him. He said he'd probably drink that day. He had somehow found the strength to not drink for the past month—a good thing because I didn't know how alcohol would react with his meds.

I had a foreboding about the weekend because when he came home from work on Wednesday, he was like a time bomb. I could feel the tension radiating from him. Thursday was no better, and when I asked him if he was okay, he replied. "I can't take much more. I'm going to kill you or myself."

I can't remember what I said, but before he went to sleep that night, he kissed me and said, "That's goodbye. I'll kiss the kids goodbye in the morning before you leave." I knew he was trying to tell me he was going to commit suicide, the final manipulation.

The next morning, he still refused to come to the July Fourth party, and somehow I found the strength to take the kids and go. When we got home around 7:30 p.m., he seemed okay, but he didn't want to go to the fireworks, so I went alone with the kids when it got dark outside. After we returned and I put the kids to bed, I waited until midnight and went to bed.

As soon as I got into bed, Joe turned and just stared at me.

"I can't do this anymore."

"Joe, you're getting help. That's a positive thing."

He calmly said, "I have no choice but to get out, change, commit suicide, or kill you."

"You're probably right," I replied, as I focused on the possibility of him changing. But while we weren't shouting or screaming, I had no idea how out of control he was until he turned to me and put his hands around my neck.

These were the strong hands I loved to watch create and build things. I couldn't move or breathe.

"Joe, let me go!" He tightened his grip. I don't know why I wasn't paralyzed with fear, but I wasn't. I could feel the pressure on my windpipe. With as much authority as I could muster, I said, "Take your hands off my neck. I can't breathe." And he did.

I was not prepared for this. I had only read about such things in books. For some strange reason, I didn't panic. In my heart of hearts, I knew Joe truly loved me in his own way. He didn't want to hurt me, but he didn't want to lose me either, and he had no clue how to prevent that from happening.

When he finally let go of my neck, I exhaled.

"Jesus Christ, I'm sorry. I'm sorry," he said and just sobbed.

I knew then that he couldn't stay in our home or he would kill me.

The next morning was Saturday, and he didn't go to work. When the kids were fed and outside playing. I told him, "Joe, you have to call your doctor and tell him what's happening. I don't think you can stay here. I'm afraid you'll totally lose control."

"I did call him, and he's off for the weekend. The doctor on call called back and told me to increase my medication."

At that point, I knew Joe had to leave, and so did he. My son, Joe, remembers to this day his dad's words to him: "Take care of your mother and Elise." After he left, young Joe remembers going into his room, where he cried and cried, not sure why or what was happening but knowing it was not good.

My husband's parting words to me were: "Once I leave, I will never come back."

Until the next day.

The Next Day

I was heading home from my mother's house with the kids. I just couldn't have stayed home that day. The night before was the first night I slept alone, not knowing where Joe was sleeping, in nineteen years of marriage. I could only hope he found a safe harbor, maybe with a friend or with his sister. Joe was very proud, not used to asking for help, and truly not thinking straight. I didn't think he would seriously consider suicide, but the possibility hovered like an ominous shadow in the back of my mind. I still felt so much love for him. I knew there was nothing he wanted more than to love and take care of me and the kids. I had no idea what was sustaining me, but I knew I didn't want to live in a prison, even if it originally had been built out of love.

As I turned the corner and drove down the hill to our house, I looked to the left on the driveway. You had to drive past the house and then turn sharply down that driveway since our house was set back down below the road. It was a basic ranch painted barn-red and set on an acre of land. The lawn was always mowed and trimmed, and there was a rose garden on the right side of the driveway and a rock garden along the left. Beyond the carport, there was a sweet stone patio surrounded by a stone wall planted with tuberous begonias. The flowers were my realm, but everything else about our house was either built, rebuilt, or expanded by Joe. I'm sure he had expected to grow old in this house, as I did.

That day, I saw Joe sitting on the front steps. *Oh, God help me*, I thought. His head was hanging down, his elbows on his knees, and he looked lost. I wanted to say to him, "Please come home. I love you. It'll be okay," but I just couldn't. This house, the kids, and me were his whole world, and I knew it. He was not lying when he said that. It must have been devastating for him to see me in the middle of all this emotional turmoil going about my daily life in what seemed to him to be a normal way. I had no time for fear. *Didn't he realize*, I wondered, *that I had no choice but to take care of the kids, the house, and our day-to-day needs, or both our worlds would crumble?* The reality that I couldn't be his whole world nor he mine must have terrified him. I'm sure he couldn't see any other life or future for himself.

I pulled into the carport, let the kids out, and walked to the front of the house. I could've cried, but I wasn't afraid. He looked like he had slept in his clothes. Looking exhausted, he said to me, "I need to talk to you. I need help. I have nowhere to go. I don't want to go to my family. I just can't. I slept in the truck last night."

"Why are you sitting out here? Why didn't you go in the house?"

"Because you threw me out."

"Please, Joe, you need to call your doctor. You need help."

"I'm gonna have to kill myself. I don't see any way out. I'm losing everything." Then he went on more desperately, "I don't want to talk to the doctor. He tells me I need to make decisions. What decisions? Change—I can't change. I need you to help me."

"I can't help you. I'm afraid you're going to hurt me."

"I would never hurt you, but you make me crazy; you make me lose control. Without you, I'm nothing."

I was lost for the right words. "I can't help you—I don't know how to help you. You can come here any time and see the kids, but you can't stay here."

I could see his anger bubbling up, the frustration. He stood up and got right in my face. "This is my fucking house! Who the fuck do you think you are? If I leave here, I'm never coming back! You better get a court order because I'm fucking coming back here whenever I want to."

Now I was scared. I was afraid of what he might do. He was not used to being crossed or having boundaries set for him. He turned, got in his truck, and backed out of the driveway and peeled up the hill.

As he did, I realized that he passed the small vegetable garden he had planted in the spring. He had planted white asparagus. They take two years to produce results. I sadly thought that crop would probably rot in the ground.

I knew I needed to protect myself and the kids. Joe told me what I would have to do to feel safe.

At this point, my family knew what a frightening situation I was in. I remember my brother David approaching me at a family get-together asking me if I was okay. He followed that up with a suggestion that he could have "Joe taken care of" if I wanted that to happen. I knew David lived on the edge, but he always seemed flush with money and influence, so he must have known some people who could take care of just about anything. Above anything else, even though I knew he was a hustler, a more-than-generous hustler, he was a family man and the protector of his family. Of course, I didn't take him up on his offer, but the threats from Joe continued.

The family protector, David and me 1982

First Step on the Path

I never liked Sundays much, and I liked them even less after Joe left—so much empty space and time. We had been separated for two months. In August, Joe went to stay with his sister. It was calm for the first few weeks. Then there were threats after threats to kill me and himself. He had also come to the house to get his guns, throwing them down from the attic to the kitchen floor. Finally, he told me in September that he wanted a key to the house so he could come in whenever he wanted. I knew that what he was really telling me was that if I wanted to feel any sense of security, I'd better get a restraining order.

That was an experience. While at times during those months, I slipped into the poor me/victim mode, I knew I wasn't going to go to court looking like the poor victim. I had lost a lot of weight over the past six months. I was so stressed that food tasted like sawdust in my mouth, and I had started smoking again. I was now a model-thin size four. I borrowed one of my mother's very expensive suits and wore it to court. I meant business, and I looked it. I don't know where I got the strength except that I still had marks on my neck from his hands. That was a good motivator.

I had never been in the courthouse, never mind in a courtroom or sworn in as a party or witness in a court case. I found that it was like being onstage during a scene in a play, but without a script and not knowing how I got there. All was quiet, all eyes were upon me, and every word was being documented. Joe's attorney grilled me on the stand, attempting to lay the blame on me for Joe's loss of control. Joe sat and watched. His eyes were black with hate. I think he felt like strangling me again, only this time he wouldn't stop. Again, the question, "What are you doing to help Joe?" He must have told his attorney that I wouldn't help him. Again, I gave the same answer. "I've been helping him for eighteen years. I'm done. He has to help himself."

I can understand why many women don't even try to use the law to protect themselves. It's expensive and intimidating to be in a courtroom full of white men in suits. Most women don't have the money and probably don't have the fortitude it takes to do it. I never anticipated I would do it either, but I've never operated on fear, and I knew my life was virtually at stake.

Chapter 14

Ho, Ho, Ho! Merry Christmas!

I *can picture myself in the kitchen* to this day that December of 1980.

My tears were falling into the cookie batter, but I just kept mixing. The tree was up and decorated. The kids were tucked in. We read *The Night Before Christmas* and sang *Silent Night*. They were so well-behaved. It's as if they knew I was fragile. The whole situation was fragile.

The wood stove in the basement was stoked and banked. Joe had vented it up through the house so it heated the whole place. He joked about the fact that he left five cords of split seasoned wood, and I've been using every log. Everything was under control. That is, everything except me. I'd been living here alone with the kids since August. So much has happened since then, and so little has been accomplished. I don't think *accomplished* is the right word. It seems to indicate that something good is happening or going to happen, and there is nothing good I can see coming from this. I expected to grow old with this man and share his social security. I couldn't stop crying and wringing my hands, but I kept making the cookies.

The kids and I got through Christmas, though traditions I thought would last forever didn't. We always had Christmas Eve at my parents with my sisters and brother and their families. The house was a small ranch, so it was a little less than cozy. It was totally chaotic with ten adults and seven kids all around the same age—three boys and four girls, and not a one shy and retiring. My mother, who thought kids should believe in Santa until they were eighteen, made it a hundred times crazier. She loved kids, any kids, but her grandchildren especially, so she pulled out all the stops on Christmas. Decorations were hung from everything that had a projection—doorknobs, chandeliers, window hardware—and every flat surface had a gyrating Santa, snowman, or elf on it, including musical accompaniment. Cacophony would be a good description, and that's before the humans were added.

We had to navigate a very narrow pathway from the door to the living room because the floor was covered with gifts piled high. Each kid had his or her own pile, and of course, they were all the same height. No favorites here. Well, there were favorites; my mother always favored the boys. I think that's because they were usually in trouble, and she loved the underdogs. My siblings and I would wend our way to the kitchen as quickly as we gracefully could to make a sorely needed drink, the first of a few—all right, of many. The kids never got past the living room, where my mother was grinning ear to ear, glowing with excitement at watching the faces of the little ones. My poor father, who wasn't exactly a curmudgeon but certainly wasn't Kris Kringle, sat in his recliner watching the crazy Christmas chaos my mother joyfully created. My mother and father were like oil and water. They only stayed married cause that's what you did back then.

Little was said of the absence of my husband—just a brief, "Are you doing okay?" Which was fine; I didn't feel like crying on Christmas Eve. But Christmas Day was another story.

For the past eighteen years, on Christmas morning, Joe's parents, Memere and Pepere, would come to our house early, too early really, for coffee. They would bring jelly donuts and honey dips from the old-fashioned local bakery and, of course, gifts for the kids. Joe's parents were older than mine, in their seventies, and had lived through the Great Depression so wall-to-wall expensive gifts were considered frivolous and a waste of money. In fact, they had spent most of their days since Pop's retirement shopping for bargains, going to tag sales, and enjoying each other and their family.

There were no divorces in their family at that point, though there were situations everyone knew of where divorce would've been warranted. I always looked forward to their visits, as did the kids, but because of the situation with Joe and our marriage, I wasn't sure how this visit would go. Were his parents angry with me for making him leave? What did they know about the whole mess? What had he told them? I was a little anxious, but I was sure they wouldn't hold it against me or the kids.

But as it got later and later that morning, and no Memere and Pepere appeared at our door, I knew something was off. At 10:00 a.m., the phone rang. It was Pepere.

"Good morning; Merry Christmas," he said. His voice sounded strained.

"Thanks, the same to you," I said.

"We're not going to be coming over this morning."

"Oh, okay—is everything all right?" I asked. There was a very pregnant pause.

"Well, Joseph told us that if we visited you, he would disown us. I'm sorry. We can't come."

Now I wanted to cry. I don't know if I was furious or just crestfallen, but I did know I didn't want them to feel worse than they did.

"That's all right. I understand, but you know you are welcome here anytime."

"Yes, and you know how he is. We won't cross him. Tell the kids Merry Christmas and take care. Bye."

He ended the call there, and I sobbed.

Joe did come on Christmas Day to see the kids. He always called to ask if he could come, which felt strange to me. I can't imagine how it felt to him. He seemed a little better when he came to the house, more like his old self. He looked healthier. I think he wasn't drinking. We're able to sit on the couch after the kids had gone to bed and talk a bit. It always ended up with us being physical. Was I interested in physical at that point? No, but this one time, I relented. What a mistake that was—in more ways than one. His visits always ended up with the same conversation.

"You know, a lot of women put up with a lot more than you had to put up with. You didn't have to throw me out."

"You tried to kill me, for God's sake!"

"Well, after what you've done to me, I can never come back here. I want it settled. I want the divorce that will make it concrete for me. I'm gonna come get the rest of my stuff, but I won't come alone because you're the only person that makes me feel out of control. You know, I really hate you. If I were you, I would be afraid. "

I wasn't terrified, but when he did come to get his stuff, including his hunting rifles, I asked my sister to come and be there with me, and I was glad I did.

The Passing of Joe's Mother

From September to January, our feelings for each other ran the gamut. He had finally gotten a small apartment in Oakville, his old stomping grounds. He would pick up the kids on the weekend and take them there. Sometimes he would come in and stay for a while, and once in December, he stayed the night. I vacillated emotionally as much as he did. I still couldn't imagine being without him for the rest of my life. Up until two years ago, this was a man I would have followed to the ends of the earth, knowing he would protect and shelter me.

We'd hold each other and cry, wondering how we got to this stage and how much more we could hurt each other, and then we'd do a 360-degree turn and agree that we needed to get divorced. It was just a matter of who would serve the papers. We tried "dating" by going to dinner together. But it always came back to two things: I couldn't live like this, and he couldn't change. He'd lose control, and I'd be terrified. It finally got to the point that he wouldn't even come into the house. He told me I should be afraid because he didn't think he could control himself. If he came to the house to get anything else, he would bring someone with him.

Then, two unexpected, tragic events happened. One made him more vulnerable, and the other put me in a position I never anticipated and made me even more vulnerable than I had ever imagined being.

We didn't talk much after he got "his stuff" from the house and told me I "should be afraid of him" until he called to tell me his mother had been critically ill at home with stomach cancer and had only weeks to live. In the next breath, he said he was anxious to move on with the divorce. We both knew that our relationship was over, but I asked if he wouldn't rather wait until the ordeal with his mother was behind him. He agreed.

I hadn't seen Memere or Pepere, the French names for "Grandmother" and "Grandfather," since Joe had left the house, but I didn't feel I could just ignore what was happening. This was the woman who always said, "Nancy, he doesn't mean it," when her only son would say or do something hurtful to me for no apparent reason. She did her best to raise a caring son despite his having a father who was an angry, somewhat violent man in his younger days, as perhaps any man was who was trying to raise and support a family during the Great Depression. They lived in a suburb of Waterbury then considered the country with no city water or sewers. Joe's mom told me that in the winter they melted snow to get water. They were people who worked and struggled to survive. She also told me once that the cat grabbed pork chops on a kitchen counter and was immediately drowned in a bucket by Pop and tossed in the trash. These were not easy times. Pork chops were not easy or cheap to come by, and hungry stray cats probably were.

Now she was deathly ill, and I had told her son he couldn't stay in his own home. I knew I had to see her, but I really wasn't sure of the welcome I would get.

Joe's family had not been at my house since he left and had even refused to come to my son's ninth birthday party on August 25. They felt it would betray their brother and son. I was crushed and knew the line had been drawn in the sand.

For so long, we had visited Joe's parents regularly with our kids every Friday night. She'd make coffee, and Pop, who by this time had mellowed into the perfect church-going gentleman, would cut up an apple every night after dinner to share. There were so many brown spots on it by the time he was done that he only had about three bites, and we would all chuckle.

Now I had to gather my courage and drive to the house they had lived in for more than fifty years, where we had had countless picnics, birthdays, Christmas holidays, and just homey family visits. What I walked into was a dimly lit kitchen and an even more dimly lit sitting room converted into a hospital room. My sister-in-law Dorothy was a nurse and had just settled Memere, or as settled as she could be. Stomach cancer is one of the most evil cancers. By the time you know you have it, it's too late, and the pain is excruciating.

Dorothy quietly said hello to me and then left the room. For eighteen years, Dorothy and I had been as close as sisters, but sadly our relationship didn't survive the divorce. There is truth to "blood is thicker than water."

Alone in the room, I took Memere's hand. It was heart-wrenching to see this stalwart woman lying in bed, clutching her now severely distended stomach. "How are you doing? Is there anything I can do?"

She looked me in the eye and said so sincerely, "How are you?" I can still cry, thinking about it.

I said, "I'm okay," and her response was, "Nancy, if the shoe doesn't fit, you can't wear it."

She never did mince words. She knew Joe wasn't living at home with me. I was taken back. What was she trying to tell me? This woman idolized her son, though I think she knew he struggled with social interactions and social settings. She really raised him herself. Joe's father was a painter and had a good job at the American Brass, but he worked twelve hours a day, six days a week. He wasn't a hands-on father, but honestly, in the 1940s and 1950s, no father was very hands-on. In fact, they were really hands-off unless the kid needed a whack. Then the hands-on was literal. It was, "Wait until your father gets home."

Now she was telling me, "If the shoe doesn't fit, you can't wear it." Did that mean, "Nancy, it's okay. You are doing the right thing"? What else could it mean? I can't say relief is what I felt, but I felt less burdened. Someone seemed to understand what I was dealing with, and this someone who was empathetic to my situation was Joe's mother! It did make it slightly less painful, at least for the moment.

The Last Blow

On February 14, 1981, Joe's mother passed, and I realized my worst fear. The one night Joe had stayed over in December resulted in my being pregnant. On the verge of divorce, two kids, no job, no money of my own, I was stressed out of my mind, ten pounds underweight, and smoking again. The irony of trying to get pregnant for ten years unsuccessfully and now it being the last thing I wanted was almost too much to bear. I had never liked watching soap operas because they seemed so far-fetched. Now I didn't watch them because my life had become one—with one dilemma after another. This wasn't a dilemma. This was a disaster.

I sat through Memere's wake and funeral knowing I was pregnant, and I wrestled with the question of whether to even tell Joe. On one hand, I knew our relationship was irretrievably over, but on the other, it was his child as well as mine.

About a week after the funeral, I went to Joe's apartment to tell him about the pregnancy. In my mind I was going to be supportive, but perhaps I was looking for support. He was calm and sad. Seeing him in this small space was heart-wrenching. It was a nice apartment, but it could not hold the spirit of this man. My sympathy for him got the best of my knowing him and how he thought. And then I blurted out the news.

"I think I'm pregnant." He looked at me as if I was crazed.

I continued, "It had to be last December." He still just kept staring at me.

Finally, he looked me in the eye and said, "How do I know it's mine?"

"How do you know it's yours!" I bellowed. "Are you kidding?"

"Hey, I don't know what you've been doing all these months. I don't know if you're going out."

I was dumbstruck. Why I expected any different response other than what I got is indicative of my continuing to hope. His reactions to me over the past year had been consistently inconsistent. I had no idea how he would react, nor did I have any expectations, but his response blew me away and cemented my decision. I couldn't see how I could carry this baby and proceed down the divorce path. This was the man I hoped would change over the years to a trusting, secure, whole person, but now he was not only insecure but also paranoid.

His response was so unexpected. I anticipated maybe anger, shock, reluctant acceptance, even sympathy—anything but doubt about whose baby this was. I could not envision myself in court trying to prove it was his. I tried to picture myself alone, taking care of a baby, taking care of Elise and Joe, taking care of the house, and supporting myself. It was inconceivable being in the state that I was. I thought about my age and the stress I had been under the past few months and made my decision. I felt the chances of having a healthy baby were not good. I didn't take the moral high road, but rather the only one I thought I could survive. I steeled myself and told my two best friends.

These are the friends who had cried with me when I couldn't get pregnant for ten years, the friends who sent flowers and made meals when my first pregnancy ended in a miscarriage. Doll was a pediatric nurse who loved babies and kids unconditionally, yet never was able to have one herself. Anne was my practical friend who arranged for me to see someone in Hartford, concerned with the confidentiality if I saw someone locally. Abortion may have been legal, but for a good Catholic woman, it was far from acceptable. It was the worst week of my life. I'm not sure why I didn't come unglued. At least I didn't feel unglued.

I don't remember what the date was but it was a bitter cold February day. I was cold on the inside as well. I tried not to think about what I was doing. What my mother would think if I told her—which I never could. I could hear her saying, "Oh, honey, how could you?"

Doll picked me up, and then we picked up Anne in Hartford. There was no conversation, no small talk other than "Are you okay? Will you be okay? Do you want us to come in with you?" "No, I'm not okay. No, I don't want you to come with me."

Anne, my practical friend said, "Do you have change if you need to call us? Here, take this dime in case."

I didn't know what to expect when I walked into the waiting room of the medical office. I didn't expect to have to be interviewed again as to whether or not I knew what I was doing and whether I was sure I wanted to terminate the pregnancy. Yes, and yes were not easy answers. They were thoughtless answers at this point, but I didn't waver. There were a half a dozen women of all colors and ages in the waiting room. Some looked frightened and tense, others stoic. A few of them were mere teens. I wondered a bit what their stories were. I was sure they were all in desperate situations. The staff acted like we were there to have a tooth pulled. Attentive, but no big deal. I had to remind myself why I was there. Why there wasn't another viable option. I then decided to numb myself to thinking and feeling about any of it for the next few hours, but you never forget.

Never.

❦

Chapter 15

It Was Final and Felt Hollow

The legal bond was broken, but I felt as though I had lost my best friend, in spite of the past few scary, gut-wrenching years.

We survived the divorce court proceedings. He looked sad and frightened, and I'm sure I looked the same. I felt sorry for both of us. As we were walking out, we made eye contact, and he asked me to go for coffee.

I said no without much conviction. I don't know what he was hoping for, but I knew it couldn't end well. It was still painful for me to imagine him with another woman, and I could not for the life of me imagine myself with another man.

We were on good terms for a while and able to communicate since he was much more stable and in control of himself. Two weeks after the divorce, he asked me to dinner for my birthday, and I said yes. It was so easy to slip back into a dysfunctional relationship. I guess that's what makes it so dysfunctional. It's not based on love and respect but rather on some sick psychological need.

It was beach time with my mother, so the kids were not around for a few weeks, and I had time on my hands. Idle hands are the devil's workshop, as they say. I don't know who said it, but there is some truth to it.

We had a decent, relatively benign but still intimate dinner. Eighteen years don't just melt away and disappear like ice cubes, but we both seemed to know we couldn't ever make it together. He admitted he didn't need me any longer because he had created a new life for himself. Of course, he had; I had the kids all this time, so my new life was on hold. I had my old life but was now alone. As my mother often said, and I still say, "It's a man's world."

Which brings me back to my brother-in-law Harry. Even though the kids were safe and sound and spoiled at the beach, their parents had to show their faces occasionally. On one of those days, when I walked into the kitchen of the cottage, my mother and Kathy were roasting a turkey—yes, a turkey, in the middle of August with no air conditioning and seven kids running around. Harry was there. He was on vacation that week, in every which way, literally and figuratively. Well, really he was always on vacation when he wasn't physically at work.

I started to help, and I don't remember what I asked Harry to do, but I do remember his response. Maybe it was to carve, except I think he considered that man's work. Whatever it was, he said, "That's woman's work." I went berserk. That wasn't the first time or the last Harry and I, to put it nicely, conflicted. I helped with dinner, cleaned up, said good night to my kids, and went home to an empty, quiet, lonely house.

I needed to build a new life, but I didn't feel the least bit prepared for that next step, nor did I have the desire to take that step. A few weeks after the divorce, my sisters asked me if I'd like to go out for a drink with them to "celebrate." I think they felt sorry for me and figured I needed practice being a single woman. They were right. We did have few laughs. A couple of guys came to our table and asked if we wanted to dance. We all said no and looked at each other with raised eyebrows, and then a guy came over and asked me to dance. I had no idea what to say or do, and I panicked; I looked at my younger sisters almost as though I was asking for permission. Finally, I put my hand on his arm and said no thanks with all the feeling I could muster and told him it wasn't personal. I don't know why I felt I had to apologize, but I didn't want to hurt his feelings. That desire to please, not to hurt, sometimes came at the expense of what I wanted to do or what I knew was best for me, especially on a personal level.

It was a very different story on a professional level. I knew what I wanted and, in fact, *needed* for financial reasons: a job. When I had worked full-time, I always found it satisfying and stimulating. My now ex-husband used to say I was a job killer because I always did more than what was necessary or expected, while at his company, if he and his coworkers put in four good hours a day, that was adequate.

Back to my finances, I had a good divorce attorney who practically begged me to take alimony, but I didn't, not even a dollar to keep it open in the future. I did accept child support at $125 a week. That's why I needed a job. I also agreed to giving Joe half of the equity in the house when I sold it or remarried. I'm not sure if it was a sense of fairness or my fear of inciting him that prompted my decisions, or maybe it was the fierce sense of independence and confidence that I would not only survive but also beyond that *succeed*.

I hadn't worked in an acute care setting for six years. True, I had worked full-time for ten years in acute care before kids, but health-care technology and techniques had changed radically. I didn't have the confidence that I could step into a hospital setting without a refresher. As always, there was the perennial nursing shortage, though, so I was able to find a four-week refresher at a local hospital with the goal that attendees would work there when they completed the course. I bought new uniforms, new shoes, and a new cap. Yes, nurses still wore white uniforms and caps. The caps used to be significant. The type and style of cap indicated what nursing program you graduated from and gave you a sense of pride. I may have been clinically rusty and slightly fragile emotionally, but I was going to look professional and sharp.

I was right about needing the refresher. Everything had changed and was continuing to change. Bedside care was no longer done by RNs. They were too consumed with managing complex infusion pumps, monitoring chemotherapy drugs, and coordinating the care for postop patients with surgical procedures not possible ten years ago. There seemed to be a prosthesis for everything from a heart to a hip. The bedside care, what there was of it, was now done by LPNs and nurses' aides. When I finished the refresher, I was offered a couple of full-time jobs at the hospital, but there was no flexibility. The kids were only eight and ten and still needed time and attention, even more so now. I watched the paper and did some networking and finally found a job in the fall of 1981 with the Waterbury VNA's nursing registry, doing private duty in patients' homes. It was not the most stimulating work, but you could pick your hours. That was critical to me at the time.

The first year that I worked part-time for the VNA doing private duty nursing in homes, I made $11,000. It was enough to supplement the child support. After six months, the supervisor of the nurses' registry offered to recommend me for a full-time position as a visiting nurse in the Medicare-certified homecare side of the company. My salary jumped to $18,000. That was the beginning of my career at VNA Healthcare.

Freedom to Choose

That first year after I was divorced, I focused on the kids. My son, Joe, seemed to turn inward. He would quietly sit in front of the very new Commodore 64 computer and eat French fries. Elise acted out, screaming and crying that I liked her brother, Joe, better than her. That was far from the truth, but I had to admit that I liked what Joe liked to do: read, write some computer code, and play Frogger and Pong video games. Elise, on the other hand, was very much like her father. She was a doer, not a watcher. She wanted to make things like potholders and macrame, turn rough stones into smooth pet rocks, and plant gardens. Her frustration was understandable. Her father would've done all these things and more with her. Today, forty years later, they are still the same. Joe says about his sister, "Doesn't she ever sit still?" and Elise says about Joe, "Doesn't he ever get tired of reading or playing video games?"

Back then, I shared my concern for both kids with the counselor I was seeing. In our sessions, he said to just keep telling the kids that I was all right, that we would all be all right, and that's what I did until we all believed it. As they say, begin with the end in mind. I also added that their father really loved them but was limited in his ability to demonstrate that love to them. I repeated that mantra to them for the next ten years, knowing that one day, they would discover their father's limitations for themselves. Eventually they did, and they accepted him for who and what he was, but they always wondered how we ever ended up married to each other.

In the divorce, I was granted full legal custody, and Joe had visitation rights. In my mind, that meant Joe could see them whenever he wanted, but officially he would have the kids every other weekend. But for Joe, every other weekend was when he saw them—no more, no less. He also gave me $125 a week for child support—no more, no less. That was his rigidity, and I expected nothing more. Joint custody was not de rigueur at the time, and if it were, I would have fought it tooth and nail. The only reason he would have ever asked for custody would be as a threat. At times, it was a balancing act doing the majority of the parenting myself, but I was blessed with the life-saving, sanity-saving support of my family and friends.

Most weekends when I had the kids, we would spend at least one evening with my sister Kath and brother-in-law Harry, having pizza and playing games. I must give Harry credit where credit is due. He was good to my kids and supportive of me and my situation early on whenever I needed it. On those game nights, we played Uno, Yahtzee, Boggle, Trivial Pursuit, Monopoly, and more. My sister still loves to play games and my kids love to play games with their kids and nieces. It was fun for all of us, and Joe and Elise clearly remember those times positively. I think those game nights sharpened their competitive spirit. Neither of them likes to lose at anything. In addition, if I needed a sitter, my mother and sister were always there for me, and I am eternally grateful for their help. It created a secure, nurturing transition from a two-parent to a one-parent family.

As for dating, I didn't date that first year after the divorce was final. But I did socialize with my friends from work, who were also supportive and understanding. They were all nurses, so naturally there was already the commonality of shared experience among us, including the fact that some of them also were divorced.

It is true that statistically nurses have a 30 percent divorce rate. The statisticians blame it on the stress of their jobs. That may be a part of it, but I think it's because most nurses have the earning potential to be financially independent. They don't have to tolerate miserable home situations so they can pay their bills. That meant that in my nursing community, there was also empathy, understanding, and no judgment.

It also meant that most every weekend there was an impromptu party at someone's house, often mine. Many of the nurses stayed at the VNA and witnessed my upward movement in the agency, and they are dear friends to this day. One of them, Linda, used to tell me that I was going to run the whole corporation one day, and she was right.

Working in home health care was a totally different experience from working in a health care institution, and I fell in love with it. There was an independence and autonomy that wasn't allowed in a hospital setting. In the hospital, there was a policy and a procedure for everything. In home care, there were some policies for technical procedures, and though there were standards to meet, you could be creative in meeting them. The patient's home was not a controlled environment, and while the nurse may have been the knowledge expert and respected by the patients, it was their home, and they were in charge. It didn't take long for a home-care nurse to learn that she had better earn the patients' trust and adapt the plan of care she developed for them and with them to suit their lifestyle and situation. It was a challenge I welcomed. An even more important factor in home care was the flexibility it provided me. If I met the productivity level each day, which I did, I was able to do my paperwork at home and usually be home when the kids were.

Of course, the kids were used to having a full-time mom in the home, but now it had all changed. I'd have to leave in the morning before the school bus came, and while Joe seemed okay with that, in my mind, I have a vivid picture of Elise hanging out the storm door in the carport crying because she couldn't do her hair by herself. Each morning when I backed out of the carport, I cried with her, but I felt I had no choice. She quickly learned not only to do her hair but also French-braid it, which was something I could never do. This scene is as vivid still in her mind as it is in mine. I knew guilt was a wasted emotion, but still sometimes it slithered in and reared its ugly head.

Actually, I didn't have time for guilt, and I had no regrets. Everyday life was busy and challenging with the kids and work. I was discovering how satisfying it was to make my own decisions and how different those decisions would have been if I were still married. For example, a few of my friends at work were planning a trip to Hawaii and they invited me along. I was forty-one years old and had never flown before. I knew it would take some planning, but I was in for the trip. Again, thank heavens for my sister Kath and her husband, Harry, who stayed at my house with their daughter, Teresa, and my kids so I could go to Hawaii without fighting with anyone about doing it. For the first time in my adult life, I got a taste of what being 100 percent myself was like without fear of starting a firestorm. It was a hell of a first flight, with a changeover in Los Angeles and eight hours in a plane, but what an experience!

We squeezed a lot into that one week—the usual Don Ho "Tiny Bubbles," Diamond Head, *The Arizona* at Pearl Harbor, and a Hawaiian luau, but I had a bit more fun than the others. They were all younger than me, but they'd go to bed way before my bedtime. I've always hated to go to bed and still do. When they went to bed, I would go down to the hotel bar and have a drink. One night I met one of the Four Tops, a famous singing quartet at the time who was performing at the hotel. We had a great conversation. Another night I met a nice guy from Australia who was recently divorced. I knew he was okay when he showed me the template of his two kids' feet he brought with him so he could buy them shoes to bring home. We talked about our kids and somehow started talking about tennis. We ended up having dinner, driving along the coast in his convertible, and playing tennis a couple of times. He was a perfect gentleman, and I was the perfect lady, so it was quite innocent, but fun. All in all, the trip was a great first-time, single-traveling experience for me and a confidence builder.

The Perfect Transitional Relationship

At some point, I began to think about dating again, though I didn't quite know where to begin. I saw an ad in the newspaper one day that an organization called "Professional Singles" was holding a dance, and if you met the criteria, you were welcomed as a guest. Supposedly, all the members were professional men and women, so it felt safe. I remember I wore a black suit and black heels. Not a business suit, but a more stylish suit with a narrow straight skirt and a short jacket with a mandarin collar. I was a bit nervous walking into the hall, but I was also comfortable with who I was and felt composed and confident. I knew that if I felt uncomfortable there even for a minute, I would just leave. I had nothing to lose.

As it turned out, I enjoyed myself. I love to dance, and lucky for me, I had many partners that night. I think it had to do with being a new face on the scene and being able to follow a good lead, something I learned from my father. That night, I met a guy I would date for the next eighteen or so months. He was the president of the club, a good dancer, outgoing, and funny. He worried about nothing and took nothing seriously. He was just what I needed at that point—and just what I didn't want for the long-term. He practically tripped over his own feet sprinting to ask me for my phone number before I exited the dance that night like Cinderella. To this day, wherever I may be, once I decide to leave, I'm gone with nary a goodbye.

He was totally smitten, and I was having fun. The wild oats that I never sowed were now being well sown. Not that I went off the deep end—I was much too responsible and focused to do that—but when I didn't have the kids, it was all about me. He fed my ego. I felt beautiful, sexy, and smart. It was the most hedonistic relationship I'd ever had, but at the same time, there was an intellectual component. We'd do crossword puzzles in bed on Sundays if we weren't doing something else. The rest of the relationship was about dinners, dancing, and weekends away to Cape Cod, Newport, Providence, Gloucester, and Block Island. The Block Island trip was storybook perfect, and I have the pictures to prove it. Jim was a professional photographer, so I have a zillion pictures of myself during the eighteen months we spent together.

We sailed with two other couples to Block Island from Old Saybrook, Connecticut, on a sleek yacht that slept six people. My brother-in-law Bruce and sister Jerilyn, who are expert sailors and seamen, leased the yacht and made the trip spectacular. Jer, who is an awesome cook as well as a sailor, did all the shopping and cooking with a little help from me. The weather was picture-perfect sailing there until we approached the port, where it was so foggy you couldn't see your hand in front of your face. Bruce had negotiated the waters with only charts, but this was scary. He asked me to stand on the bow and shout as soon as I saw the docking area. I swear it appeared when we were about two feet away from it, and Bruce had to throw the yacht in reverse or we would've landed with an unwelcome thud. We dropped anchor away from the dock so we could take the dinghy into the island at night. There also were some scary dinghy rides back to the yacht after drunkenly singing our brains out at the piano bar. It could've become a Natalie Wood drowning situation, but we all were able to struggle back on to the yacht without going under—but just barely.

I knew my relationship with Jim was going to be short-lived. It was the perfect transitional relationship for me—no stress, no pressure, no responsibility, and no commitment. He did come to family events, picnics, and holiday gatherings, but he was never going to be considered family. My mother raised her eyebrows a few times. My kids didn't like him, and I didn't blame them. He was

Block Island, here we come.

into me and not the kids. He was a single parent, a widower with two kids. One was a son, who left home at sixteen, and the other was a thirteen-year-old daughter who had cerebral palsy. She was left on her own most of the time with some hired help, which did not sit well with me, especially when I realized that my fun times could have been at her expense. When I did break up with Jim, he was heartsick, but I knew he would be fine. He was a survivor and would find a way to continue to enjoy life, albeit irresponsibly.

Part Three

Rebuilding

Chapter 16

A Workplace to Thrive In

As much as I loved being a visiting nurse, it didn't take long to realize that how we documented our work was onerous and duplicative. It took longer to document what you did for the patient than it did to do it, which meant nurses completed their paperwork on their own at home after hours. It seemed to me that if we could dictate our admission documentation, it would be quicker for a clerical person to transcribe it than for the nurses to handwrite it.

This was the first project I volunteered to work on. My co-workers felt that they didn't have time to volunteer for projects and sometimes resented that I did, but I was able to envision a better way to work and that motivated me to find the time. A data entry person and I piloted the project with the permission of the director of the agency, Donna, who was a forward-thinking young woman, a graduate of Yale, and one of my first mentors who gave me opportunities to develop skills outside of the nursing compo-nent of my job. When I presented the data of the pilot to her, she was impressed and said she would talk to the office manager about expanding the project. Not realizing my success was about to get me into big trouble, I was thrilled . . . until a couple of days later when Donna called me into her office. When I walked into her office, I could tell by the look on her face that this was not going to be pretty. She immediately lit into me. When she presented the data to the office manager, the office manager hit the roof and lit into Donna. She was livid because she had been left out of the loop during the pilot, and you know what they say about what rolls downhill in an organization. This was my first lesson, learned the hard way. If you hope to create positive change in an organization without stepping on toes, you must include all the shareholders, everyone the process touches, every step of the way, especially if it's a function or process they're responsible for. The office manager was responsible for the data-entry function, and I, in my ignorance, had not included her. It wasn't the last organizational lesson I learned the hard way. I made peace with the office manager—*mea culpa, mea culpa, mea maxima culpa*—and we implemented the dictation solution.

Another lesson learned from this first opportunity repeated itself again and again throughout my career. It was that most human beings are inherently resistive to change, even the ones you're trying to help. Some will fight it outwardly and blatantly, which is manageable and not necessarily destructive, but there are those who will go underground and silently undermine and sabotage any change to the status quo. You must hope they are not the sacred cows in the organization who for some reason are protected by an influential manager. As I moved up in the agency, I came across both types. Fortunately for me, along the way I educated myself in organizational behavior and developed the skills to work with, through, or around both types.

The next opportunity that came along was to pilot and implement a new role in the agency.

It's become clear to me that when I'm competent, confident, and comfortable in my job, I tend to start looking for a new challenge. It seemed to happen every three to four years. In the ten years I worked before having children, I had worked on med/surg, the ER, Labor and Delivery, the OR, and Long-Term Care. I had been a visiting nurse for four years in 1985 when I saw the job posting for a VNA/Hospital liaison nurse and applied. This position was not only totally new to the agency but also to the health-care system in general. There was no written job description, just the concept that this VNA nurse would work in conjunction with the hospital discharge planners to ensure a safe, effective transition of the patient to home. This would be the chance to enhance the transfer of correct information from the hospital nurses and docs to the VNA nurses—the correct meds, diet, activity, and follow-up care.

I interviewed for the job with VNA managers and hospital managers. During one interview, Donna asked me if I would be willing to back up the position if I didn't get the job. I don't know where this came from, but I said, "No. I want the job, but not as a backup position." This was one of the first jobs I interviewed for and got without the preferred education and credentials. A bachelor's degree in nursing (BSN) was preferred over a three-year RN diploma from a hospital nursing program, though the state board of exams for licensure were the same for both. I knew I would have to go back to school at some point and get my degree, but the timing wasn't right now with two young children and a full-time job.

This was a lateral move for me financially, but it gave me the opportunity to create something innovative and challenging. Money has never been a motivator for me, but it was always a welcome result. The director killed two birds with one stone and asked me to write the job description for the new role. She not only saved herself from having to write it, but also gave me more ownership of the role. The new position also gave me an opportunity to work at St. Mary's, the hospital I knew well, and to renew relationships as well as develop new relationships with important referral sources for our agency. I also met a couple of single young women at the hospital who asked me if I would like to go out with them on Friday nights to September's, a local restaurant and bar where they had Friday night singles dances. They told me they knew this nice guy they thought would be perfect for me.

Let's Try This Again

I had been single for five years. I wasn't looking to be married, but I did miss the company of a man, especially the aroma of a nice cologne. I love the scent of a man. In October 1985, off to September's I went with my newfound friends from St. Mary's, and they introduced me to Tom. He was a good-looking guy, well dressed (all his shirts were monogramed with "TLC"), engaging, and quick to smile. The bonus was he used Paco Rabanne cologne, and to top it off, he was a very good dancer.

The first few Fridays I went, we danced and talked. He had been divorced twice and had three kids with his first wife who were around my kids' ages and lived with their mother. His story with the first wife was that she met someone else and wanted the divorce. He was well over that. The second wife, also a nurse, he divorced due to issues with their kids. She had two boys whom he thought were spoiled and trouble, and his kids thought she was a bitch and couldn't stand her. That was that. I didn't see any pattern or warning signs, so forward I went.

Tom and I were about the same age and enjoyed many of the same things. He was the first guy I knew who enjoyed shopping, cooking, and housecleaning. He was also very good to his kids and seemed to like mine, and they liked him, both important factors for me. For a few months, we would meet at September's with the group, but soon we began seriously dating. I would get flowers and romantic cards for no reason, but interestingly, as romantic as it seemed, I was the one who initiated our sexual relationship and maintained it. I didn't see that as a red flag. Would you?

After about seven months, we talked about marriage. We had met each other's families, and he had met my friends. He passed the "I like him" test, though one friend wondered if he might be an ax murderer because he seemed too good to be true. I knew he wasn't an ax murderer because he was a clean freak and would never make that big of a bloody mess. Neither of us felt that living together was an option. I don't think it was from a moral perspective, but more of what kind of an example it would give the kids.

Tom was spending most of his time at my house, and finally my daughter said, "Why doesn't he just move in?"—which he did. Tom, like a good roommate, did his share of everything, plus when he ironed his five shirts every Sunday night for the next week, he also ironed my blouses. You couldn't beat that. He was an accountant for a local manufacturing firm, so he wore a suit to work every day; a college-educated man was also new to me. He liked clothes and treated himself to very nice things and kept all those things nice. He was very structured and methodical, as accountants typically are. It was a nice change from laying out a man's clothes and being 100 percent assigned to a woman's role when it came to managing a household. I didn't think that was a red flag either.

We set the date of April 19 for our wedding. Tom had a small tax business and did taxes on the side, so nothing of any import occurred on the weekends during tax season until after April 15. We decided to get married at my home since it was the perfect setting for a wedding (thanks to my ex-husband!): a spacious yard and patio and an in-ground pool outside of the bar and rec room. I had hosted my sister's second wedding reception at the house, so I knew it could work.

We spruced it up a bit with painting and some landscaping. We did it ourselves and probably overdid it because two weeks before the wedding, I bent over to brush my teeth and felt something pop in my back. I had herniated a disc in my spine. Bad backs are an occupational hazard for nurses who are constantly lifting and lugging patients who can't move themselves. I ended up in bed for two weeks being waited on. The timing couldn't have been worse.

I felt this could change everything. I knew I didn't want to have surgery, though I had constant pain and numbness down my left leg, because most of the spinal surgeries I had seen were not successful for the long-term and led to more surgeries. I decided instead that I would do physical therapy and yoga. I had taken up yoga after Elise was born, and I knew I could strengthen my back and core and thus manage my back pain. *Knew* may be a strong word; I *hoped*.

Two very respected doctors, a neurosurgeon and an orthopedic surgeon, told me that without surgery, I wouldn't be able to walk, much less play tennis or golf, but they were wrong. I was determined. With the unknown outcome, I was unsure if Tom would want to commit to marriage, and I asked him outright if he would like to call off the wedding. I was really prepared for any answer, but his response was loving and supportive. The wedding was on.

We were married by a minister friend in a simple ceremony with close friends and family attending. It was a great party despite the fact that the servers I had hired didn't show up, and two of my "gold" friends, Anne and Doll, ended up working their buns off. There was plenty of delicious food, and the liquor flowed freely so no one else really noticed. These are the same two friends who supported me through every crisis, including life and death situations, and enjoyed every celebratory event with me; they are my friends for life. Doll said she was exhausted and that this better be my last wedding because it was the last one she would attend. Anne was so drunk driving back to West Hartford that she begged God to let her get home safely and promised to never drink again. As she tells the story, the minute she walked into her house, she made herself a drink! So much for bargaining with God.

Tom and I settled into marriage comfortably. I can't remember if I articulated it, or if it was an unspoken agreement, but he kept his boundaries with the kids. I wouldn't tolerate another man disciplining my children. Thankfully, the situation never arose since they were both basically good kids. They liked Tom, and in every other way, he treated them as he treated his own children. Joe felt that Tom was a good role model, and Tom and Elise had a good relationship. My son tells me to this day how lucky I was that neither of them even thought about stepping out of line.

Both good students, Joe was a sophomore at Holy Cross, and Elise would be going there next year after graduating from middle school. Education has always been important to me, so I opted for a private high school for them. Not that I had money to throw away, but I clearly remember my mother saying education is something no one can take away from you. I wanted them to have every advantage to live healthy, productive, satisfying lives. Their father didn't agree and felt public school was adequate, so it was my decision alone, and I would pay for it. Joe was still so very angry and stayed that way almost until his dying day, when he finally said, "I have to admit you did a good job with the kids."

Tom and I stayed in that house for a couple of years. He was a good housemate, as I've said. He did his share of the household stuff, cleaning, cooking, grocery shopping, laundry. But he had no interest or desire to take care of a yard or an in-ground pool in the summer or to shovel snow or be stuck in a steep driveway in the winter. He wanted out of the house and into a condo.

I had managed the house by myself for six years with a pool, yard, driveway, the kids, and a full-time job. But I've learned over the years that, in personal relationships, I tend to not want to make waves (also a gift from my mother, albeit a questionable one). Tom and I didn't have a prenup, but we did decide that his money was his and mine was mine. We split the household expenses in half, including the mortgage and taxes, but the house was mine, and of course, all the kids' expenses and tuition were mine. That was never an issue until they got to college and needed financial aid—the divorce before the divorce story. At this point we were making about the same amount of money, although I may have been making a little more.

Tom was easy to live with as long as you didn't touch his stuff, which is probably why he put his initials on everything from his shirts to his leftovers. Once Joe, an oblivious fifteen-year-old at the time, ate Tom's leftovers, and he nearly went berserk. From that day forward, Tom initialed all his leftovers. We stayed in my house on Sherwood Drive for three more years. during which time Tom was let go from his accountant job for reasons unbeknown to me and struggled to find another one for months. As a last resort, he took a job as a headhunter for a firm in New Haven, Connecticut.

I knew nothing about head-hunting. I was more familiar with being hunted for jobs, but I learned quickly it was primarily cold calling and a lot of sales work. Tom had to generate his business from nothing and was paid on commission, which was very stressful especially when Tom commuted an hour to work each way. Tom was tired from the job and so consumed with it that he convinced me we should find a condo and sell the house. As per my divorce decree, I had to pay Joe 40 percent of the current value of the house when

I remarried, so it was mine to sell. My sense of justice sometimes outweighs my common sense.

The house went on the market, and we started the search for a condo. The timing was good. My kids were in a private high school so they wouldn't be uprooted, and my career was growing and consuming more time. I had also started back to college part-time to pursue my BSN; my master's would come later. My goal was to get those degrees before my kids did. I did it, too—but barely.

The housing market was good in the mid-1980s, so I sold the house for ten times what it had cost twenty years before. We found a great condo in a new development in the west end of Waterbury, near the kids' high school. The units were two-level duplexes, very roomy and bright, with three bedrooms and space for Tom to have a small office for his tax work. Tom continued to struggle as a headhunter, while I, on the other hand, was about to apply for my first supervisory job as a home health aide supervisor. The liaison position I had initiated was fully established in the hospital, and I was ready to move on. When the new opportunity in management arose, I took it.

A Taste of Managing Change

The homecare aide, who works very hard for very little compensation, is the person who provides the most intimate care and support for a patient and their family. I felt they needed more training, more support, more recognition, and more input into how they did their work, so when the opportunity came to make improvement in those areas, I went for it. I was also pragmatic because it was the only supervisory role in the agency that didn't require a BSN, and I hadn't earned that yet. I had no idea then what doors this would open for me in the agency and in the world of cutting-edge technology in home care. I learned, in a very painful way, that the cutting edge is also the bleeding edge when you're a first implementer.

I got the job, and luckily for me, another home health aide supervisory position opened up, and a nurse I knew and respected as a visionary and a change agent got the job. Iona Watterworth was one of the first nurses to work directly with cancer patients receiving intense radiation to shrink tumors when there were so many unknowns, and she instituted and developed the VNA hospice program almost singlehandedly.

When the AIDS disease was barely acknowledged in 1980s by anyone, she saw to it that at VNA, we took care of young men dying of AIDS at home. She trained a few brave HHAs in their care and then had to practically beg morticians to pick up their bodies when they died. She was fearless. Young gay men, ostracized by society, came home from New York, Boston, and California to be with their families to die. Iona's was the only hospice home-care program that would accept and care for these patients.

I was thrilled that we were now working as a team to hopefully improve the status of the aides and thus the care of the patients. Our supervisor, who was the first in a long line of sacred cows I came across, was not going to be easy to manage. Another skill I learned on my career path was managing up, which is a little more complicated than managing down. You must be slightly more subtle so your superior doesn't recognize being managed, but instead sees it as an opportunity for him or her to look good. Another valuable management lesson: Always make your boss look good.

Our supervisor had been with the VNA for years and years. She was an intelligent, soft-spoken, compassionate nurse who wouldn't recognize an organizational wave if it washed over her, never mind make one. But administration loved her. She did her job, caused no trouble, listened to problems and issues, and never did one damn thing to resolve them. I used to say she came to work every day (she was also reliable) and it was like she was starting from scratch. There was never an initiative, a plan, a project, or a different result. The same thing day in and day out—numbing!

It didn't take her long to realize that Iona and I loved to make waves, and there was going to be a tsunami. There was no issue brought to our attention that we didn't think we could fix. We videotaped orientation and new education programs so the aides could watch them anytime. We were often in trouble for pulling aides out of homes that were unsafe or where they were being verbally abused.

The biggest wave yet to come was a technological opportunity a Yale professor presented to the company CEO.

The CEO of the agency, Peg Cushman, was a brilliant, entrepreneurial young woman who would ultimately move our small VNA, through mergers and acquisitions, forward to become the largest VNA in the state and one of the largest and most influential on the national scene. She also became my mentor for twelve years of my career. She was a Yale grad, and when Marc Schwartz, PhD, also a Yale professor, approached her to work on a project to implement a telephonic electronic time sheet and care plan that would be computerized for the aides, she sent him to our boss. Our boss handed that project over to me so fast it was like the hottest potato in the pot, and I leapt at the chance. I could picture the outcome in my head and knew how I could make it happen. My partner in crime, Iona, was also happy to hand it over to me. We made a good team; Iona was more clinical and patient-focused, and I was more organized, process-focused, and outcome-oriented.

Over the years, Iona and I became good friends and shared our personal as well as professional lives. She was the first person I mentioned my concern to about what was happening in my marriage to Tom. It wasn't that we weren't getting along—we were—but our relationship had become platonic. It was either too early, too late, or he was too tired or too stressed for sex.

She passed it off, saying, "That's bound to happen after a few years. I know he loves you. Give it time." So, I did.

A Seismic Shift from Nursing to Information Systems

That HHA documentation project paved the way for my next adventure into the world of information technology, the new wild frontier in health care. I worked with Mark to develop the beta version of software system, developed the training manuals, and completed the pilot. I found my inclination to always seek improvement in most any arena was fed by the obvious efficiencies that valuable outcome data that computers offered. At the time, the only computerized processes were finance, so naturally the only reports and data that could be gathered were financial. In the early 1990s, Medicare was attempting to find ways to measure clinical as well as financial outcomes, but without data it was a lost cause. Our CEO knew that if she were going to get any meaningful clinical data out of a system, she would need a clinician in the information technology world, and I was ready to learn something new.

The new role she envisioned was an RN systems analyst, and it was mine if I wanted it because no one else applied internally or externally. It was a role that could only be imagined since there was no model for it, but I could picture it. I was supercharged because somehow I knew that technology was the key to future solutions and pathways to clinical and financial success. What I didn't realize early on is that the greater the scope of the challenge, the more people needed to manage it. I could not do it alone. I, for some reason, had always had personal power, whether based on knowledge, integrity, trust, or something intangible. Up to this point, though, I had no formal organizational power, but I was able to initiate small, focused organizational changes and implement them. An agency-wide conversion from a manual documentation and data entry billing system to an automated integrated computerized system was neither small nor focused. It would impact every department, every employee (all 1,300 of them), and every business function. There was no stopping now, and I was soon to find out that my new role was a key component of the initiative's success or failure.

I was in uncharted territory. What I had undertaken is now called "health-care analytics and informatics," with project management thrown in. I knew no more about flow charts, computers, coding, hardware, software, alpha testing, beta testing, and new system implementation than the man in the moon, but the project for automating the home-care aides care plans and telephonic time sheet that I managed was successful, so I guess the CEO thought I could manage this groundbreaking endeavor. I must've thought so, too, because I accepted the job.

But another lesson I learned is that there can be collateral damage to what seems like a positive change. There was an outcome to that HHA time sheet/care plan project that no one had anticipated. It was a financial impact—and not a positive one. The electronic time sheet reflected to the minute when the aide arrived and left the home. It might not match the schedule of two hours or four hours, but it was how we paid and billed. It took months to figure out why receivables had decreased and many man hours to resolve the issue of reconciling the discrepancies. I didn't get off on a good foot with the chief financial officer, and it never got better, even when we were on the same senior management team, but I knew more about his world of finance than he knew about my clinical world, so we were on equal ground.

I was about to learn the hard way how little I knew about what I didn't know and the unanticipated results of system changes. Lucky for me, the agency had just hired Dave, a young computer guru who had not only the techie component but also could relate to users as well. I was old enough to be his mother, but he became my technological mentor. Talk about baby steps! He helped me create my first ever password: "adminrn." I occasionally use it to this day but with an additional number and symbol. Four years later, I was made the manager of IT, and I became his boss and mentor.

I relocated from the Waterbury office to the central administration office in Plainville, Connecticut, where he and I sat in tiny cubicles adjacent to each other. This office housed all senior management, the president and the vice presidents of the agency, as well as shared services such as IT, payroll, and human resources—and me, the lone clinical person. The agency now consisted of three major branches and three small offices with 1,300 employees. In addition to commuting from Waterbury, I was also traveling the country.

The leaders of the ten largest VNAs in the United States put their heads together and decided that in their agencies, they had the skills and intellectual equity required to develop and write their own software for a home-care clinical documentation system—or at least the ability to identify all the critical components it needed for an RFP. As a result, they put together a group of clinicians from across the country to form a work group to identify and document all the components of the system. Every month, one of the VNAs would host the work group for a three-day session in their home state. I was identified as the brain trust from our agency, and for a year, once a month I traveled from Connecticut to Buffalo, New York; Santa Fe, New Mexico; Long Island, New York; Atlanta, Georgia; New Orleans, Louisiana; Chicago, Illinois; and from Connecticut to San Diego, California. What a trip in more ways than one! For someone who hadn't flown until she was fortyish, I made up for lost time and experiences. I met strong, assertive, intelligent women who were fearless change agents and dynamic, opinionated risk takers. I was as much in my comfort zone intellectually as I was out of my comfort zone technologically.

In anticipation of the enormity of the change, the CEO created a new director of information systems position and hired Mel from IBM. Mel had supposedly managed complex installations and implementations in the business world but knew nothing about health care and less about home health care. Dave and I were Mel's minions.

Mel also was part-owner of a liquor store one block away from the agency. It took Dave and me about three months to realize we were in big trouble. Mel was spending more time at the package store and had no interest in learning about home health care. It took the CEO about six months to figure it out, and Mel was gone.

In that past year, as I was learning about systems, hardware, and software, and database development, I discovered that the IT staff had their own language that did not translate to clinical staff and vice versa. It dawned on me that I could now speak both languages fluently—clinical to the IT geeks and "tech talk" to the clinical staff. It dawned on me as well that the finance people had their own language. It took me years to learn that, but they never learned clinical. They didn't think they needed to. That hasn't changed, which is one of the reasons why the health-care system has crashed and burned today.

Later, Mel's job for information systems director was posted. Guess what? I applied. Yes, I applied. I'm not sure what I was thinking, but I had learned the strengths and weaknesses of everyone in the systems department—the programmers, computer operators, database managers, and payroll processors (one of whom was a sacred cow, a silent saboteur, and an eventual thorn in my side). After all, I was an RN. I was trained to observe and assess, process info, diagnose the problem, develop a plan to improve, and get the patient on board: management in a nutshell. The hardware was still a mystery, but I knew technical staff who could help me with that. During the previous year, I had worked with all the IT staff to help them be more successful in understanding and meeting user needs, and as a result, they were getting positive feedback instead of complaints. They trusted and respected me.

The CEO was a maniac when it came to data. When Peg wanted a report, she would send a request to the database manager in her language, the database manager would come to me and ask what the hell Peg was asking for, and I would explain what data fields she needed to pull. So, when I interviewed for the IT director position, I mentioned that to Peg. She admitted it was the first time in years she had gotten meaningful reports and was willing to give me a chance as the acting—"acting," not "actual"—director of IT. It was understandable that I had to prove myself; after all, to date I had never taken a computer course. I was ready for the challenge.

We had finally selected the software vendor after months of site visits and deliberation. Implementation of the new Electronic Health Record (EHR) agency-wide was imminent. The term *EHR* is still used today.

If I had known what lies ahead, I would've have been terrified.

From the Frying Pan into the Systems Fire

Failures are not always mistakes.

I'm struggling to put into words the massive undertaking the implementation of EHR was for the agency, but especially for me. The good news was that with my new position as manager, I now had formal power. The bad news was that with formal power comes serious accountability (i.e., "the buck stops here"). I was now the project lead having never managed a project at all, much less one of this size. Just for perspective, I'll list what I was ultimately responsible for:

- Project scheduling and road mapping
- Data migration and data cleansing
- User training (at least four hundred staff) and change management
- Testing and go live activities
- Security assessment

I was also indirectly responsible for:

- Hardware and network upgrades
- Productivity loss
- Data backups and storage

Do I need to describe what a near catastrophe this was? It took months to convert records, cleanse the data, and teach and manage the new processes with resistance and frustration at all levels. The employees were expected to do their jobs while spending hours learning how to give up paper and trust a system that was unforgiving when it came to errors. For months, we could not get bills out the door, and as a result, cash flow was a serious issue. The impact on me was working day and night at the frontline granular level with a small group of die-hard stakeholders who trusted me to fix it. I would go to the kids' sports events at night with work in my lap. I lost ten pounds and developed an ugly case of stress-related rosacea.

And don't talk to me about irritable bowel syndrome! Luckily, I had a physical outlet since I had continued playing tennis year-round with my tennis partner and now friend of forty years, Kathy. I've remained physically active throughout my life with yoga, tennis, golf, walking, gardening; I was always moving, and for that I must thank my father. It has saved my sanity many times.

It took at least a year of relentless toil and trouble to get the company back on an even keel. Senior management was supportive of me and my staff primarily because they could not afford to have me fail. A failure would've brought the agency to its knees. After leaving a senior management meeting where I had given an update of the dismal status of this project, the VP of the private duty side of the agency pulled me aside as I was walking to my cubicle from the boardroom. She looked me in the eye and said, "You know you can do this. I know you can make this a success."

I sincerely thanked her and never forgot her encouragement since I wasn't getting much positive feedback at that point. She was a smart cookie, a little rough around the edges, but also a personal friend of the CEO. I knew she was a good person to have in my corner.

Unfortunately, the clinical staff who looked to me for direction, support, and advocacy was disappointed. Their ability to do their work suffered during the conversion, and I had lost their respect and trust. That was tough for me. I was always invested in them, and I remained invested in them. Thankfully, I had the opportunity to prove that I had their backs when I moved into a clinical leadership role in the next few years.

I learned more from this near total failure about people, management, and what it takes to create positive change than I learned from any of my successes past or future. This near failure didn't discourage me from seeking more and more responsibility, though it probably should have. When all was said and done, the CEO looked at this as a scary success and proof that I could manage systems, so she made me not only the director of systems but also director of quality management with the understanding that I would go back to school and finish my BSN degree. I don't know how I worked full-time and went to school part-time, but I did. I got my BSN in 1993, barely ahead of my son getting his undergraduate degree.

Chapter 17

Divorce before Divorce

Through all this stress and angst, Tom, always the good room-mate, remained stalwart and supportive. He never complained about the long hours or the travel and stepped up with housework and cooking. I remember being at my friend Anne's holiday party in West Hartford, sitting on the couch with a couple of women; Tom was standing behind the couch talking to a couple of guys. I'm unsure of the gist of the conversation, but I heard Tom say that one of the things he liked about me was that I made my own money. That stuck in my head as a heck of a thing to say, and it always stayed in the back of my mind. The fact that I made so much money, especially when added to his, would come back to haunt me when Joe started college.

My son, Joe, was a freshman at Boston College in 1991 when I received a letter from the financial aid office that Joe wouldn't receive any financial aid because my husband, Tom, and I made too much money. While Tom and I were filing our taxes jointly, I was paying 100 percent of my children's education. Off I went to Boston

College with a briefcase full of receipts, cancelled checks, mortgage statements, and whatever other paperwork I thought would help prove that I was financially independent of my husband, but to no avail. The tax statements were what financial aid was based on, and they were the bible to the financial aid office. I had eight more years of college to manage, since for two of those years I would have two kids in college. I could only see one solution, and that was divorce.

Again, Tom understood what I had to do. He was as pragmatic as I was. Or maybe he wasn't invested enough to care, I'm not sure. But when I approached him with what I felt I had to do, he said he was okay with it as long as I paid for the divorce. That also stuck in my head.

Thus, it was the divorce before the divorce. It was bizarre, I guess, and we didn't tell anybody, not even the kids. We went through the six-hundred-dollar process to end our marriage, but since our relationship could not have become more platonic than it already was, our daily lives continued as usual.

Maybe the platonic relationship was a good thing, and I just didn't recognize it as such since I didn't really have to invest a lot of time in it. Of course, that could be the "chicken and the egg" enigma. Did it become platonic because I didn't invest enough time, or did I not invest time because it became platonic? I did invest some thought, though. When I raised my concern to Tom that he kissed me hello and goodbye the same way he kissed my friends hello and goodbye, he didn't see it that way and said he was content with the way things were. Perhaps I should have been. We socialized together, cooked together, cleaned together (though he was probably doing a little more housework than me), and he still ironed my blouses along with his shirts for work.

There were no arguments, no friction to speak of, but there was also no intimacy or passion. Sometimes, in retrospect, I wonder if

I should've just had affairs along the way and let the marriage exist as many do for practical reasons like shared expenses and shared meals. There would always be someone to go to a movie with, someone to give you a ride or shovel you out if you were stuck, or even someone to carve the turkey. I did live that way with Tom for about five years—but with no affairs.

I should probably be grateful that my marriage to Tom, though boring, was stable and didn't require much energy physically or emotionally. He continued to be very supportive of my career advancement. I'm sure we still looked like the perfect couple. I would say we truly had mutual respect, and that probably came across to others. We didn't bicker or bad-mouth each other ever. There was never a lot of drama, just quiet acceptance.

In the meantime, Tom was in survival mode at his headhunter job. Because of the stress, the commute, and the financial tension, he was always looking for a change, and he eventually found an accounting job with the City of Waterbury. The pay was all right, and the benefits and the potential for a vested pension after ten years were very appealing. Tom wasn't looking for a job to be challenged or on the cutting edge of anything at this point, but slow and steady worked for him. He still had his income tax business on the side, which was all-consuming during tax time, and he began to get involved in the workings of our condo association, ultimately being elected the president. He was perfect for the job—slightly compulsive about rules and a financial conservative.

The last thing I wanted to do was be involved in condo business, and personally I hated the rules. In fact, I was thinking about buying another house, not that I needed more space. I had recently dropped off Joe at Boston College; I literally sobbed all the way home, soaking tissue after tissue and barely able to see to drive. It was one of the most heart-wrenching things I've ever done. My heart healed quickly, though, after about two weeks. Elise was then a high school senior and would soon be heading off to Boston University herself. That transition wouldn't be as heart-wrenching, since by that time I knew they were both just a two-hour drive away from Connecticut.

The kids' college years flew by. They were both in Boston, making it easy for me to visit, even just for lunch. Like high school, I never had to worry that they weren't doing what they were supposed to, or else they were so good at covering up any problems that I never found out. They both tell me to this day how lucky I was. Drugs or alcohol were never a problem for them. I remember being in Boston for a conference; I was staying at the Copley Hotel when I got a call from Elise. When your child calls you sobbing, it's never a good thing. She was on campus living with three roommates.

She sounded desperate. "I can't stay here. It's too noisy. I can't study or sleep. Can I come stay with you tonight?"

"Of course, how will you get here?"

"I'll take the T."

Then I waited and worried. *The T (the Boston subway)? Does she know how to find me or what T to take?*

But, of course, she did and arrived at my hotel room door within the hour. We were both relieved and glad to see each other. The crisis passed, and she settled in, but off campus.

A Taste of Travel

During Joe's first year of college, he lived in a house on campus with other students who had like interests, and he adapted easily to the experience. He majored in French and International Affairs, something he had wanted to do since he was in middle school and had a French teacher he liked. He had the opportunity to spend his junior year in Nantes, France, and this gave Tom and me the opportunity to visit with him there.

Over the years, Tom and I had bought a couple of time-shares that he was able to trade for two condos on the French Riviera near Cannes. Tom had his strengths, and one was dealing with the dirty details of time-share ownership and getting the biggest bang for your buck. Thus, the day after Christmas in 1993, Tom, Elise, and I left for Paris to meet up with Joe with a treat he wasn't expecting. We brought with us an Italian grinder from one of his favorite delis, double-wrapped in foil and only slightly bruised from the trip. He savored it!

We stayed in Paris for a few days and did the usual tourist stuff, including the Eiffel Tower, the Champs-Élysées, and Notre Dame. I say the usual stuff, but it was anything but usual. It was eye-opening and mind-opening, as well as mouthwatering. We enjoyed croissants and café au lait, warm baguettes with soft brie cheese, filet de sole Beurre Blanc, and always a bottle of wine. It helped to have a French speaker in Joe, immersed in the culture as our guide. My son, in fact, found my American dress of jeans and sneaks slightly crass. Then, when we were served a pizza with a fried egg in the middle, I chuckled, and Joe was also not happy. He said my behavior was rude.

So, I was on my best behavior when Joe's French host family asked us to have dinner. It wasn't easy to pick out a bottle of wine to bring to dinner where wine selection and tasting is an art. There we sat on French provincial chairs in the small formal dining room, struggling a bit to communicate with Joe translating. When Madame served a soup that was thick and green, Elise gave me a sideway glance that said, "I can't eat this," and I gave her a look that said, "Just spoon it in or else," which she did.

Tom was able to book us two condos on the French Riviera close to the Italian border for the last week of our vacation. Joe was going to meet us at the station to take the fast train from Paris to the town of Menton, the Pearl of the French Riviera. As we waited in the station, we watched the letters and numbers on the board that posted the destination and arrival time for the trains move so rapidly it was dizzying. We also watched the arrival time to board the train come, but no Joe. Tom, Elise, and I looked at one another. What should we do? My stomach was in a knot, thinking first, *What the hell happened to Joe?*, and second, *How were we going to negotiate our trip with very limited understanding of the French language?* We finally decided we would board the train and hope he would make it. Today, we would have just called his cell.

There we sat on the train with the engine running as people boarded, and now I was slightly panicked. Everyone was settled in, and the conductor was collecting tickets as the train slowly started out of the station. I didn't know whether to cry or puke. I should have been more confident that eventually Joe would have gotten to us. After all, he had managed himself here for the past four months, but a mother worries. The train was speeding along, not lumbering like the Long Island Railroad. We were flying by skinny cows in a field, when the door to our car opened and in burst this tall, thin, handsome young man with dark curly hair just like his father's.

After I said, "Thank God," to myself, began to breathe normally, and my heartbeat slowed, I said, "Where the hell were you?"

"I'm sorry. I overslept and just made it on the last car. I walked through all the cars until I found you." Even Tom was relieved to see him.

It was a six-hour ride to Menton, the lemon capital of the world. It's a beautiful coastal city, lush and warm year-round with fragrant flowers hanging from walls and trees full of lemons everywhere. It's a small town, so we were able to walk down the narrow winding steps from our condos in the hills to the main road along the coast of the Mediterranean.

There were shops, grocery store, cafes, and sandy beaches. We walked across the coastal path from France to Ventimiglia, Italy. We shopped, cooked, and ate together at our condos for New Year's Eve as we watched the show at the Moulin Rouge on television—not a bad gig. The next day, we took the train to Monaco, also a magical place, and did a little gambling in the casino. All in all, it was a memorable trip, and the first and last one we did as a family with Tom, so something to cherish.

Whether it was just the three or sometimes four of us, we were always solid as a family. I was twice blessed with both my kids who never gave me one ounce of the typical grief kids can bring into your life. Though through no fault of their own, they did give me a wicked scare one Christmas Eve. We were all at Tom's daughter Diane's home in Bristol. Joe and Elise had driven there separately so they could leave early and go to their dad's.

This had been the routine since we had divorced. Their dad would see them early on Christmas Eve, and then they would come to my mother's and meet up with us. My son, Joe, and Elise, who was driving, had left Bristol to go to their father's house and been gone maybe an hour when I got the call from Bristol hospital that my children had been in an accident, and I needed to get there as soon as possible. I still feel sick to my stomach writing this. Tom and I drove there to find my son, Joe, sitting in a waiting room, seemingly unharmed. He had not been examined yet, but when he was, they would find his abdomen and chest severely bruised by the tightening of the seat belt at impact. Then they took me into the examining room to see Elise. She was not unharmed. Her skull was split open to the bone from her scalp to her right eyebrow, and her clothes were covered in blood. Her right wrist was broken, and she was being monitored for a head concussion.

All my adult life, I never panicked during a crisis. In fact, the more serious the situation, the more grounded I got. I was calm as they stitched Elise's scalp closed and set her arm. But when I saw Joe's bruised body, I was crazed. The cops told me they had been hit head-on by a drunken woman with two drunken men in the car. Did the driver get hurt? I don't know, and I didn't care.

Tom and I took the kids home. I got up every hour to wake Elise to check her blood pressure and her pupils to be sure there was no cranial pressure, and I checked Joe to be sure he was breathing easily. Elise was out of school for a solid week, missed her senior year basketball season, and she ended up with a large scar on her forehead that remains until this day. Of course, the car was totaled.

New House, No Relationship

Tom and I lived in the condo during the kids' college years, but I still wanted to move back into a house. Tom wasn't interested in moving to a house, so I started a search on my own. It was fun. I would have liked a big old house like those in an older section of Waterbury, but Tom dug his heels in on that one. I still looked at them, though; they had such character. I also looked at a big old house in Woodbury, Connecticut, with an octagonal barn, but Tom, the fiscal conservative, nonrisk taker, said it was "too big, too hard to heat, too much work, too far out." I finally found a house I liked in a good section of Waterbury, right up the street from my parents. The real estate market was somewhat depressed in the late 1990s, so it was very affordable. In fact, I wanted to keep the condo as an investment and rent it, but Tom said it would only be a headache to manage. I listened to him, and that was a mistake. In hindsight, I could've managed it quite well.

The new house was called a California ranch, meaning it had an open concept layout, large windows, and was L-shaped. It also had an interesting history. It was built in 1956 by the students at Kaynor, the vocational high school Joe went to in the mid-1950s under the guidance of their teachers. All the work was done by student carpenters, electricians, plumbers, and welders, and it was very possible Joe had worked on the construction when he was a student there. Tom wasn't sure about the house, but he came along, reluctantly at first, but then he seemed to think it was a good move. Of course, at this point, I could afford to have all the burdensome chores done, so neither of us had to worry about those. We moved into the Clough Road house in 1997. Our relationship was unchanged: platonic, uneventful, and predictable. Well, maybe not so predictable—I guess it depends from whose perspective you're predicting.

It was a sunny Saturday morning in May 1999. I remember it clearly because I was sitting at the dining room table looking out the wall of windows to the backyard. The forsythia along the border of the yard were in full bloom, the branches of the lilac bushes toward the back of the yard were hanging heavy with flowers, and right outside the window, I could see the daffodils and tulips breaking ground. I always sat at the head of the table on the left because I could see the whole room as well as the yard. This was a great room in every sense of the term. The modern Drexel fruitwood dining room set we had bought for our first house in 1964 was at one end. Furniture then was made of real wood, and brand names meant something. This furniture lasted forever and never went out of style. I'd had fifty years of family holiday dinners at that table, anywhere from ten to twenty people, and I finally donated it when I downsized in 2018 for the final time.

At the other end was a brick wall the width of the room with a fireplace and raised hearth. This was the sitting area, and smack in the middle of the room between these areas was my concert grand Baldwin piano. Off and on as an adult, I had taken piano lessons. When my father passed, he left me some money that I shared with my brother and sisters, but when my piano teacher told me she wanted to sell her piano, I figured that was a good use for the money I had, and I bought it. It sits in my living room as I write this, and someday my son will own it, and then hopefully my granddaughter will want and appreciate it, but who knows. Legacies don't seem as valued these days.

Anyway, back in 1999, I was having coffee when Tom came in to have breakfast. I wish I could say that we had had some raging battle or at least a major disagreement, but I can't. I just knew this was not a relationship I wanted to stay in. The sameness and the lack of intimacy, spontaneity, and affection were just not worth having the company of someone in the house. I can remember telling my mother when she was in her sixties and seventies and justifiably complaining about my father that she should divorce him. She would say to me, "Honey, it's somebody in the house." Well, I'd rather be lonely alone than lonely with somebody in the house.

I don't think Tom said anything as he sat down, but I said, "You have to leave."

He said, "You're throwing me out?"

Not "I love you," or "Let's try to work on it," or "What can I do?"

"You have to leave," I repeated, and he did. That's how simple it was to end a ten-year marriage.

He said, "I'll gather my stuff and call my son to come help me. I'll get the big stuff this week, if that's okay."

By that afternoon, he was gone along with his kitchen knives and spices. That was it. I went to say hello to his son when he came to help with heavy stuff. He and I had always gotten along, but there was no hello, just icy silence. I'm sure it was upsetting for his kids. How could they understand when there was never any drama or craziness? They knew this was his third divorce, so I don't think they were too shocked. Maybe a little drama or craziness would have made it more interesting and lasting. Remember, we didn't have to get divorced. I had already paid for that when Joe was in college.

That Monday, I went to work—same old, same old. Nothing really felt like it changed in my life except there was no one to make dinner or eat it with. No one at work knew for months that I was alone until Tom no longer came to work social events and someone asked. I can't say they weren't surprised. I had told the kids, who at this point were no longer living home. They were a bit shocked but accepting. I told my friends, who were now mutual friends of both Tom and me. They were like, "WHAAT?" As I've said, everything appeared perfect, and maybe on some level it was, but on many levels, it wasn't for me.

Professionally, my life was a different story.

Chapter 18

Building a Career

My role at the agency continued to expand from focused responsibility for localized areas to overall company responsibilities. For example, I took on Quality Management (QM) for all clinical operations across all regions and offices.

When I stepped into this role, I had to back into the formal requirement of a master's degree, which I agreed to get within a two-year period (and did). I also had no formal training in Quality Management, so I researched, studied, and documented the QM theory and concepts and presented on the topic to the senior management team and staff in all five locations. As part of the senior management team, I now participated in strategic planning and had input on decisions made at the highest level impacting every employee up and down the organizational structure.

Thanks to the foresight of Peg, our CEO, the timing couldn't have been better to implement a QM approach. The federal government agency overseeing Medicare had begun developing their tool (*OASIS*) for measuring outcomes and costs in Home Health Care

(HHC). At the same time, the agency was transitioning from a quality assurance approach that involved doing chart reviews to assess retroactively that the right steps were taken to a proactive approach to quality through established protocols with measured outcomes.

I learned so much during the next five years from both research and Peg. She was not only forward-thinking, but she also was a management guru who believed business cultures could be created. Every year before our annual strategic planning process began, she would give the vice presidents their required reading. This material included not only statistical and financial information on the status of the agency but also the most current management theory books that focused on positive organizational change.

The books I particularly remember reading included *Strategy of the Dolphin* and *Systems Thinking* and *The Fifth Discipline* books by Peter Senge. Others were *Think Out of the Box* and *Raise the Bar* by Mike Vance. Vance was the dean of Disney University and had worked with Walt Disney to create Disney World and a culture of creative thinking. He also wrote and developed a management tool called *Displayed Thinking* that I used to manage people, products, and projects for my whole career. Vance used a nine-dot matrix to plot the necessary components of a creative culture:

- People, Place, Product

- Involving, Informing, Inspiring

- Caring, Cooperation, Creativity

Mike Vance had worked not only with Disney but also with Steve Jobs at Apple and Jack Welch at General Electric. Thanks to our CEO, Vance worked with our management team and our industry over a period of years. This experience and exposure to successful management theories prepared me with applicable strategies not only to succeed myself but also to help others succeed. I made it easy on myself to foster people's advancement by always hiring people who were smarter than me or who knew much more than I did about the job for which they were hired. That practice, I believe, ensured everyone's success.

I enjoyed the Quality Management role where I learned how to collect data, convert it to useful information, and then apply it to implement improvements in our services. But I sorely missed the clinical operations side of the business. That work impacted patient care directly and provided an opportunity for me to work closely with the nurses and other clinical staff.

So, in 1993, when I had the opportunity to apply for the position of director of the Waterbury VNA , I went for it. By now I had gotten my BSN and a master's degree in Health Care Administration, so I didn't have to "back into" the educational requirements—a new experience and a pleasant relief. When I interviewed for the first time for this new position with the CEO, who had already seen and appreciated the results of giving me two opportunities based on my energy and passion for positive change, she noted that I really didn't have much clinical operational experience for this job other than managing home health aides. I thought, *Here we go again!* But I knew I could do the job, and I convinced her to give me the chance based on my past successes. She ultimately agreed.

Just about twelve years after my friend Linda's prediction, I was returning as the director. Linda still reminds me of that!

There were so many advantages to having this new role. In addition to the office being five minutes from my home, I knew all aspects of the city, its people, and the surrounding towns, having lived there all my life. There was another bonus: Everyone there knew me, trusted me, and respected me, and the feeling was mutual. For the past few years, they had an acting director who was a former educator at Yale with no home care or operational experience. The next director, who had held that same position in the Hartford branch, was relocated to Waterbury. She was very nice but couldn't affect the change that was necessary there.

When I got the job, the staff in the Waterbury branch welcomed me back with open arms. There was a large reception in the office boardroom, with all the staff present, of course, but also friends and family, city dignitaries, the state representative for the area, and other community business leaders. But what really warmed my heart and moved me was when the home care aides came in from the field to celebrate my arrival. If anyone knew my investment in people and my management style, they did. I could tell they were as thrilled to have me back as I was to be there.

A Change of Scenery

My life wasn't all work and no play at that job however. While I don't have much gypsy in my soul and am a nester at heart, I have done my share of travel. Sometime traveling seems like so much work when you could just sit in your cozies in your living room and read about any place in the whole world with accompanying pictures. But my lifelong friends and supporters, Anne and Jo, both love to travel—imagine, *love* not *like* to travel—and occasionally they convince me to join them. For about twenty years, we traveled together to Hilton Head Island in South Carolina, but I call that vacation, not travel. It's a great recreational spot I still visit every year.

Usually we fly to the island, rent a car, and stay at Palmetto Dunes, right smack in the middle of the island. Everything you could want to do on vacation is there—golf, tennis, beaches, pools, kayaks, bikes, and of course, eating in good restaurants. It is always relaxing and revitalizing to go there, especially when my work life was intense, stressful, and almost all-consuming. Thanks to technology, I was never far removed from the day-to-day of my job, so I savored the temporary escapes to the island. Occasionally my traveling friends would convince me to explore Beaufort or take a ride to Savannah to sightsee, but most days after golf and dinner, I was content to be home and read or watch television, unlike my friend Jo.

Jo and I had been friends since sixth grade—through high school, nursing school, marriages, divorces, and beyond—so she knew my family intimately. Even when she moved to Boston to live and work, we never lost touch. We weren't soul sisters; we were more like "opposites attract," but I never thought anything would fracture our friendship. I was so wrong.

Jo could be an itch; she was totally unorganized, never ready on time, and always losing stuff. She was never very respectful of shared space when we vacationed together, which could be annoying, especially to our other friend Anne. For instance, Jo set up the ironing board from the moment we arrived and there it stayed until the day we left, smack dab in the middle of the dining area. Because Jo was never ready, Anne and I were the ones to cook, clean up, and load the car, but we dealt with all of it because she was our friend and had a good heart. She was also a fighter who had struggled twice with breast cancer, both times without a complaint. We all had had our struggles: illness, divorces, kid problems; but Jo had a loss that cut deeper than anything Anne and I had to deal with.

Jo's mother, who had been a nurse, died giving birth to her. Jo didn't talk about it often, but I think that kind of early loss, especially of a mother, leaves a vacuum in a person's life that no one else can fill, not even a father or a sister. Even her doting Aunt Molly couldn't compensate for it; she literally gave up her life and left her home in Ireland to came to Waterbury to take care of Jo and her siblings. I was always willing to cut Jo a lot of slack because I realized the blessing I had in my mother's love and sympathized with Jo for what she missed.

Still, there was another issue that was trouble in so many ways. Once Jo started drinking wine, she didn't stop. One night after dinner at the Marriott, a hotel close to us, I was more than ready to head home. I had had enough to eat and drink and was tired. Anne and I were taking an early ferry to Daufuskie Island the next morning for an early tee time. We could hear the music coming from the hotel lounge, though, and I knew what was next.

"Let's just have another drink in the bar," Jo suggested. "Maybe someone will ask us to dance."

"Jo, I'm done. I'm heading home," I said. "If you want stay, I'll walk home. It's not far."

Anne chimed in, "I'm out too. We have to get up early in the morning to catch the ferry at 8:00 a.m. Just take us home and come back."

Jo agreed to that. She came in maybe an hour or so later, feeling no pain, as they say, and went up to bed with another glass of wine.

Six-thirty the next morning came quickly, and by 7:30 a.m., Anne and I were dressed, fed, and ready to go. We loaded the golf clubs in the car. It was a little chilly but bright and sunny, perfect for a ferry ride and eighteen holes of golf at the ocean course. I slid into the driver's seat and turned the key, but nothing happened—not a *whirr* or a *purr*, just silence. I looked at Anne, and she looked at me, slack-jawed. It was obvious to us both that Jo had left the headlights on all night, and the battery was stone-cold dead. No Daufuskie Island golfing for us that day!

We were so angry we could hardly speak, and what we did say isn't printable here. Of course, there were multiple apologies from Jo, and eventually we got over it. But that wasn't the straw that broke the camel's back when it came to my travel friendship with her.

A few nights later, after dinner at the condo where we were staying and again after too much wine, Jo wanted all of us to go out. We were barely over the dead battery, and I was adamant.

"Jo, I'm not going," I said, as I got up to make a cup of tea.

Jo shot back at me, "You're just like your mother. All you want to do is stay home and do crossword puzzles."

I was stunned. Jo had spent hours and hours at my house when we were growing up. She knew my mother. Anne looked at Jo and then at me. She knew Jo had crossed a line. Jo knew it too.

I responded to her in a flash. "You know what! You have a hell of a nerve, berating me and my mother. I am so done."

I walked out of the living into my bedroom, shaking with fury. She had hit a nerve, and I made a decision . . . a difficult decision.

We got through the next few days, and before it was time to leave, Anne made it clear to Jo how upset I was. But even Anne didn't realize that would be the last time Jo came to Hilton Head with us.

Anne kept asking me, "How will you ever not invite her?"

I had no idea, but I had decided my downtime was too important and life was too short to be criticized for my personal choices while on vacation.

Jo finally found the perfect spot for herself. When she retired, she sold her house in Boston and bought a place in The Villages in Florida. The Villages was made for Jo. You could drive to the square, of which there were many, in your golf cart. They had music and dancing most every night, and you could get two glasses of wine for the price of one. She loved it.

When we'd talk on the phone, she'd say, "You have to come visit me. It's awesome. Everyone dances, people with walkers, women alone. We can go out every night. There are all kinds of clubs to join, and lots of golf."

I was happy for her. She made new friends who enjoyed the same social life as she did, and I was totally off the hook. We remained friends until she passed in 2017, but we never vacationed together again.

After that trip to Hilton Head, I started my new job as director of the Waterbury region. Although I thought it was my dream job and I had reached the pinnacle of my career, there was much more to come. But I have to say this Waterbury job set me up for the future and taught me some invaluable lessons as a manager.

First, in every organization, politics comes into play. There are always people whose *modus operandi* is political. They focus on who has the power, how to please them, and how to use the resultant allocation of their power over you to become more powerful. But I had no time for politics. I had dealt with it at a minor level in previous roles, but usually with rational dialogue and some give-and-take, I could get around the politics.

However, in my new position as regional director, politics became more of an influencing factor, if not a determining factor, in decision-making. I learned to play the game, but I was never quite comfortable at it. My mother would often quote Shakespeare and say, "To thine own self be true and then it shall follow as day follows night, thou can't be false to any man." At risk of stating the obvious, it is very difficult to stay true to yourself in an extremely political arena. In my experience, flip-flopping is almost a prerequisite.

Politics became even more of an issue in the mid-1990s when I was made an officer of what was now a $40 million company with three Medicare-certified home health-care branch offices in each region, a private duty nursing company, a managed care company, and a Durable Medical Equipment (DME) company.

This job was an important move in my career because it positioned me to have an even more influential position of greater fiscal responsibility and stewardship. I was one of six vice presidents who made up the management team reporting to the board of directors. Being at a VP level in the company expanded my circle of influence and formal power, but at the same time, I had to confront many more complex political situations.

When I was director of the Waterbury region, my direct fiscal responsibility and managerial scope was for only for that region, where I could easily oversee and manage the financial aspects of the business, the revenue, and expenses. I didn't always agree with the approaches of the other directors in their regions, but their decisions didn't affect me and my reputation directly. Now, as a vice president, they did, and it was a dilemma for me. The CEO had close personal relationships for years with three of the other vice presidents before they advanced to those jobs. Were they bad people? Definitely not. But the CEO did lean more toward their input and opinions in decision-making than other vice presidents, including me. That was not a well-kept secret in the company, yet no one was going to say something out loud. I walked a fine line for five years managing the situation because I loved my staff and the work.

At times, I spoke up when my thoughts and perspectives differed from the other vice presidents, but I did so cautiously. Occasionally, I also would vent to the vice president of Human Resources, who was also aware of this troublesome dynamic. I would meet with him regularly to discuss personnel policies, and occasionally I would mention staff in other regions asking to meet with me on unresolved management issues outside my region. They did this because they knew I was not one to ignore or bury a problem, and I could usually find a path to do the right thing for patients, staff, and ultimately, the agency.

When I raised a specific serious issue to him, telling him I couldn't let it lie and that I needed to find a way to raise it to the

CEO in a nonthreatening way, his response was very clear. "Nancy, stay in your own sandbox." I did for the most part, and I managed to stay under the radar when coaching staff from the other regions on how to manage up to influence and make change.

Peg, the CEO, despite some bias toward certain personnel, was a strategic guru who taught me more about strategic planning than if I had been an apprentice to Jack Welch. She was always ahead of the curve in most aspects of the health-care industry and foresaw the development of large vertical and horizontal health-care systems years before they happened. She was a mover and shaker in our industry, and I wanted to be part of that. Together, we merged with and acquired smaller agencies, developed a managed health-care company that established contracts with vendors, and became part of a large hospital system. We soon became the largest VNA in Connecticut and one of the largest in the Northeast, other than New York City and Boston. We focused on patient outcomes and the pledge that "not one visit more or less than necessary would be used to achieve the desire outcome for the patients." That was our strategic vision. This was all good, at least to the naked eye, but it also was an important statement since the reimbursement methodology for Medicare and Medicaid was still fee-for-service. That meant that the more visits you did, the more money you made. Even though Peg knew the payment methodology wasn't going to stay fee-for-service forever, she didn't foresee that reducing visits would cause severe financial damage for our agency in the short-term.

True to our strategic vision, we continued to decrease visits per episode, and as a result our billables and revenue decreased. As anyone who is business-minded knows, to survive in that scenario requires cutting expenses. But rarely can enough expenses be stripped out of a highly regulated government-driven business to cover the income loss, so we began to lose money—at first, a drip-by-drip loss.

At the monthly board meetings, the financials would be questioned, of course, and Peg would explain that this strategy was going to prepare us for prospective payment in the future versus fee-for-service. Somehow our CFO was also able to rationalize the losses and present financials that were approved by the board. I had taken lead in the agency in a Medicare-driven, prospective payment pilot project, and our data was good. Our patient outcomes met Medicare criteria even with fewer visits per episode—an episode being from admission to discharge.

But unfortunately, we were so ahead of the curve that by the time the federal Health Care Administration had finally implemented a prospective payment system many years later, we had lost millions. Everyone knew that Peg wouldn't be there forever, and around this time, she decided to leave. She was an academic at heart and wanted to pursue her PhD and other avenues. I believe she resigned thinking she was leaving the agency on solid ground and well prepared for the future.

When the search began for a new CEO, I realized that new leadership could mean a whole new management team; it would be a monumental change, not only for the agency but also for me. Still, I had no idea of the crisis that lies ahead, and even if I did, I would have stayed and faced it head-on. I have never operated on fear of the unknown, and I wasn't going to start then.

This was 1997, and both my children were now self-sufficient. Joe had finished his master's degree in education at Harvard University and was teaching high school in Virginia Beach. He was also playing and coaching beach volleyball—not a bad life. Elise had a master's degree in physical therapy from Boston University and was working at St. John's Hospital in Santa Monica, California, where she had done a clinical internship. She was also doing personal training and playing some volleyball herself. Although Joe did sow some wild oats in Virginia, I didn't have to worry about either of them.

What a blessing that was because when the new CEO came on board, all hell broke loose, and I had more than I could handle at work.

The Rothberg Era

There were many applicants for Peg's position as CEO. It was appealing to anyone who was running a small operation and wanted to move into a leadership role in a larger agency that seemed positioned for the future. The board and senior management decided to hire Ellen Rothberg, a young woman from Boston, also a Yale graduate. Ellen was as different from Peg as theory is from practice. What I learned from Peg in theory was invaluable, and I applied it throughout my career, but what I learned from Ellen in practice was just as valuable. She had experience with startups, for-profits, and not-for-profits and was more financially savvy than any nurse I knew. When she came on board as CEO, she interviewed each of the vice presidents. So, when she interviewed me, I got a chance to get to know more about her as well.

I had read her resume, but I was more interested in her management style than her list of accomplishments. Evidently, she knew about my background in IT and my project management experience there, so she was interested in my role in the agency and how I got there. When she asked about the management team in general, I trod very carefully. She was a bright person and, to my mind, would soon figure things out for herself. We ended our meeting with her telling me to be patient, give her time, and lay low.

It took her about one month on the job to figure out that the agency was in a deep financial hole and not much more time than that to convince the board, who were incredulous at first and then shocked when the hatchet fell. It took about three months for Ellen to change the whole management team. The first to fall was the CFO, then the VP of the private duty company, the DME company, and VNA Managed Care. Subsequently, the VP of the Hartford region left on her own when she saw the writing on the wall. I kept a low profile as Ellen had advised me earlier, managed my areas of responsibility, and took care of my business.

Ellen was smart enough to not involve me until the dust settled, and when we finally met, she informed me that I was now responsible for the whole kit and caboodle. She asked me if I was willing and if I thought I was able to do that job. I said yes with some trepidation because I knew the undertaking would be an enormous responsibility.

At that point, my salary jumped to a new six-digit number. Ellen thought I was underpaid, and for what she was expecting of me, I was. I won't say there wasn't pressure; there was plenty. I knew nothing about running a DME company or a managed care company. Once again, I was out of my comfort zone, but I could envision what needed to be done and thought I could do it with Ellen's direction and guidance. I was willing to grow.

And grow I did. The following two to three years were painful, stressful, and full of consultants. In total, we had had a $7 million loss, and we had to turn the agency around as soon as possible or it would go under.

The first step Ellen took was to get rid of the businesses we knew little about, which were managed care and durable medical equipment. That was the easy part, and then we refocused on our base business, home health care. The wicked hard part was cutting to the bone expenses that affected every employee, from vice presidents to home health aides, and all benefits including health insurance, pensions, and salaries. Every department and process had to be examined for waste and redundancy. To this day, I still remind Ellen of what that did to my pension, and we laugh about it. The most problematic issue was finding a way to communicate to staff what was happening. Ellen was relentless in her approach to getting the agency on solid financial ground, for obvious reasons. We went from office to office and presented the dire situation to staff, looking for understanding and their buy-in to what needed to happen. I was on board, but my emotional investment was greater than hers since I knew every employee personally by name, from the managers to the home care aides. I valued them as individuals and coworkers. They were key components of my success, and it was gut-wrenching.

Ellen was a networker, a deal maker who could be political when necessary, and she was able to work with banks and the health-care system to restructure the debt. She knew which organizational experts from around the country to bring in to help us, both financially and structurally. We established best practices and set benchmarks. Then we established operations groups to monitor the benchmarks and adjust accordingly with smaller work groups.

Ellen was all the things I wasn't. I didn't like networking, deal-making, or politics, but I knew operations management and quality improvement practices. I knew how to take a plan or project from step one to completion and be flexible when necessary. I knew the agency and its people so intimately that I knew how to get staff on board, and I used the *Inform, Involve, Inspire* method I had learned earlier in my career to do so.

Ellen and I made a good team, and it all worked out. Of course, there were moments, more than once, when I thought from an emotional perspective, *I can't do this.* I wouldn't say that during this process golf saved my life, but it gave me a diversion that cleared my head and helped me to take a deep breath and relax my overworked brain. I left my clubs in the car, and often I would just go to the course after work and walk nine holes alone. I'm not sure what Ellen did to cope, and she would occasionally "lose it" if someone didn't quite get it. It was not a pretty sight, but for the most part, we both stayed calm and single-minded. We focused on our core mission of serving patients and eventually turned the agency around after months and months of restructuring the management team, consolidating departments, and streamlining processes.

None of it was painless or easy for anyone, but it was critical. I officially retired when the agency was back on its feet and financially stable. Ellen was not one to withhold her praise or appreciation of what had been accomplished. She nominated me and I won a leadership award from the National Organization of VNAs, and when we would attend national conferences, her colleagues would always approach me to tell me how highly Ellen thought of me and my leadership skills.

Travel Is Not So Bad

Managing a non-for-profit health-care organization is never easy, but at least now that we were not in crisis mode, I was able to think about taking a break and enjoying a change of scenery, or maybe some travel.

My dear friend Anne, the traveler, wanted to go to Italy and asked me if I would go with her. Her timing was perfect because I felt like I deserved a reward for a job well done.

The lure of European travel had tempted me before the Hilton Head Island incident with Jo, so she and I had traveled together to England. Her brother Jackie and his wife were living in London at the time, so we stayed with them. Jackie was a civil engineer who, after graduating from the University of Connecticut, worked and traveled all over the world until he settled in London with his wife. Staying with them gave me a sense of a different lifestyle from the one that I grew up in. Everything in their flat was small, including the kitchen, the fridge, the stove, and the rooms. London was a vibrant city, but at the same time, it was staid and historic. We saw *Mamma Mia* in the theater there and visited all the traditional sites, including the Tower of London, the Changing of the Guard at the Palace, 10 Downing Street where the Prime Minister lived, and the Parliament. We also took the train through the Chunnel between England and France, making our way to Belgium and enjoying a formal dinner on the train.

The whole experience in England did whet my appetite a bit, so I was looking forward to Italy with Anne. She had been to Italy before, but not to Sorrento and the Amalfi Coast where we wanted to go. We planned a trip with Gutsy Women Travel, an agency that did worldwide tours for women only. That kind of travel appealed to both of us. We had been single for many years, and while we did have some couple friends, the dynamic was different with a group of women. The conversation always seemed more authentic and the laughs more heartfelt and natural. This proved to be true on this trip.

There was a mixed bag of women—sisters, mothers and daughters, groups of friends, and a couple of married women who came alone because their husbands didn't travel. There was only drama one morning at the hotel breakfast when a couple of women from New York complained that they couldn't get an omelet. The tour guide, Gabriella, was mortified and tried her best to please them. It was an embarrassing American moment at a bountiful Italian breakfast.

The Mediterranean coastline was breathtaking; seeing it and feeling it beats reading about it. Making gnocchi at an Italian cooking school was also more fun than watching it be made on the Food

Network. The cranky, portly chef for our lesson made me throw out my first batch of dough and start over. I handled it too much, she said in a not very nice tone. While in Italy, we ate our fair share of pasta and fish and drank more than our fair share of wine and limoncello. We walked the Isle of Capri and entered its blue lagoon on a crystal-clear day. There were also days of just hanging in the palazzo with a cup of cappuccino and soaking up the sun and the warmth of the culture.

The Amalfi Coast, Anne and me

Anne had been to Rome before, but I hadn't, so we decided to add another week to our trip after the tour and go to Rome. I was excited about it for crazy reasons. I wanted to see the catacombs and the Colosseum. I had studied Latin for four years in high school and translated Caesar and *The Iliad*, so I had a good idea of the history of the Roman Empire. But it was really Russell Crowe, the movie star, and before that Kirk Douglas, as gladiators that moved me. I love gladiators. If I were to put myself back in history, I'd be a slave girl in love with a gladiator! But that's another story.

Rome wasn't part of the tour, so we were on our own, and Anne made all the arrangements. We took a train from Naples to Rome; the cab driver who took us to the train station spoke very little English but just enough to warn us not to let go of our pocketbooks or bags in the train station. He said there were pickpockets, thieves, and beggars with "fake" babies. By the time we got to the station, we felt like we were in mortal danger, but we discovered he wasn't exaggerating.

We sat on a bench, clinging to our belongings, until the train pulled in. As we got up to board, we must've let go of the bags for a split-second because an American guy approached us and warned us again. He told us how he had been robbed of everything—his money, his passport, and his luggage. We listened wide-eyed as he helped us on the train.

While in my experience, Naples is everything everyone says it is, Rome was everything I expected and more. We stayed at a small hotel, The Hotel Cecil, right near the Spanish Steps in the heart of Rome, where we walked to a small brassiere for breakfast. We wrestled with the idea of a formal tour of the Vatican or just exploring it ourselves with the help of Rick Steves, the travel guru and author of guidebooks all over the world. We went with Steves.

Little did we know what a fortuitous choice that was. We were so blasé. We got up that morning, had our breakfast, and then took the bus from the Spanish Steps to Vatican City. I chuckle now when I think back on it. We had no idea what we were doing. We got off at a little variety store in Vatican City when Anne said, "I need to get film."

I was like, "Really? Now?"

"Yes, you never know. I may want to take pictures."

So, there we were, standing in Vatican Square in front of the Basilica, watching all these robed people walking about, including priests, nuns, prelates, seminarians, and a group of tourists with the tour guide holding up a flag so her followers wouldn't get lost. I took out Rick Steves's Rome guidebook and looked up Vatican City. I never looked up from the book again for the next two hours.

The book, which became our bible, said, "Do not go into the Vatican right off. You can see the Pieta later. If you see a tour group, just attach yourself to them and pretend you belong."

I read this out loud to Anne, and we joined the tour with the lady with the flag. No one noticed. We followed the tour past the line waiting to get into the Basilica and entered the Sistine Chapel. It was very impressive. We sat on the skinny stone benches and looked up at the ceiling at a stunning depiction of scenes from Genesis: Adam and Eve to Noah, three hundred figures in all with glorious colors and movement. This was an "OMG" moment in the literal sense.

The tour guide talked a bit, but we didn't listen because our guidebook said, "Leave the group now and go into the apse of the Basilica," which we did. It still said leave the Pieta until later. In our benign ignorance, we did what the book said.

We walked up to a lush red rope strung across the entrance to the apse in front of the main altar of the Basilica that prevented us from getting closer. The Basilica was huge, with a high ceiling that seemed to reach to the heavens. I put the guidebook aside for a minute as we took it all in. Soon we felt, rather than saw, people coming behind us—many, many people. They were just standing behind us until we noticed that suddenly there was activity in the front and to the sides of the altar. Something was happening up there.

We looked at each other and decided we weren't moving. We couldn't have moved anyway because at this point there were one hundred people behind us. Then we saw the television cameras and microphones being placed and sound checks being done. Choir boys were lining up into the left of the main altar. There were official-looking men in formal dress with swords—maybe the Swiss Guards?—who came up to the lush red rope and asked all of us if we were there for Mass. Of course, we said yes. They released the rope, and we walked into St. Peter's Basilica to the first nonreserved row of pews. Anne and I took a seat with three nuns on our left. To our right was the aisle leading to the altar.

I finally asked the nun on my left, "What's the Mass for?"

"One of the pope's housemen," she said. "He has passed, and the Mass is for him."

Now a slew of bedecked bishops came in and sat to the right of the altar. That's when we noticed the poorly disguised security guards dressed in suits, very well fitted to their well-muscled bodies, with earbuds and mini mics, checking everything and everyone out. It was all very serious.

Soon, the poor soul's family dressed in black, the women all with mantillas on their heads, came down the main aisle and into the reserved pews directly ahead of us. When the organ music started, the choirmaster raised his baton, and the young boys started singing in sweet, prepuberty voices. We heard a shuffling of feet behind us, and everyone turned to face the center aisle.

We followed suit as the processional started coming down the aisle next to Anne. She pulled out her camera with the film she thought she might need, and I guess she did need it, because Pope John Paul, in his little red shoes, appeared in the middle of the processional right next to us. Anne started snapping pictures. It was then we realized that the pope was the celebrant of funeral Mass for his houseperson. Anne and I looked at each other and started giggling, the kind of giggling that you can hardly control. The nuns looked askance at us, so we pulled ourselves together.

My friend Anne, who would never want to be dressed inappropriately for any event, turned to me and whispered, "Thank God we didn't wear jeans."

We sat through the entire Mass in awe. The pope gave the sermon in Italian, of which we did not understand one word. We both received Communion, in my case sacrilegiously. I've been excommunicated from the Catholic Church so many times!

When the Mass and the recessional were over, Anne and I waited until almost everyone left. Then, as Rick Steves's guidebook had informed us, we now had the Basilica just about to ourselves, with plenty of time to view the exquisite Pieta as well as St. Peter's tomb and the dome over it painted by Michelangelo.

As we sat on the bus heading back to the Cecil Hotel, we couldn't stop talking about our fortunate opportunity and what a story we had to tell when we got home. We tell it to this day and chuckle.

I am grateful Anne was able to motivate me to see Italy as well as convincing me to take a trip to Spain. She's still trying to convince me to go to Ireland, but for now, the little gypsy in my soul is satisfied. But I must confess: I did fly to Tampa, Florida, one weekend a month from 2002 to 2004 . . . motivated by love.

Blessings

My daughter, Elise, and her husband, Todd, were living in Tampa, Florida, where he was doing a fellowship in oncology when she became pregnant with my first grandchild. I was in the fortunate position of having a boss, Ellen, who allowed me the freedom and a career that provided the financial wherewithal to fly to Florida at least one weekend a month to spend time with Elise after she stopped working. Todd was very committed to his work, so she enjoyed the company and diversion.

I didn't really try to arrange my time in Tampa with Elise and Todd so I could be in the delivery room for Brendan's birth. How could I have planned to travel across the country to beat out labor pains and nature's plan? But Providence intervened.

I was sitting in the Bradley airport in Hartford late in the morning on Friday, December 10, 2004, waiting for my flight to leave, when Elise called to say she was in labor. Todd was taking her to the hospital and would pick me up at the airport when I arrived. I couldn't believe my good fortune. Three hours later, I was sitting in labor and delivery with them both as Elise was about to deliver. Elise had spinal anesthesia, so when Brendan Alekshun was born, he was the most bright-eyed, aware newborn I had ever seen. It was as if he were saying here, "Here I am, what's next?" And it's been "what's next?" ever since.

I was privileged to be there for his first bath, his first words, and his first steps. Both Todd and Elise were very generous with their new son, probably because he could wear one person out in a New York minute. The child was never still unless you were reading to him, but even at that, the story had to be fast-moving and animated. He wasn't even a good sleeper. He fell asleep quickly enough, but he would wake by 5:30 or 6:00 a.m. If he awoke in the middle of the night because his diaper was sopped, we tried not to make eye contact with him because he'd be standing there, waiting expectantly, ready to get up for the day. We had to just pick him up, lie him on the changing table, change the diaper, and toss him back in the crib. No eye contact, no chatter, nothing that would engage him.

Providence intervened a second time when my granddaughters were born three years later. Todd's fellowship was just about over, but Elise was pregnant with twins and had to fly home a few months before he was done, or she would have been stuck delivering in Florida. She and Brendan stayed with me for those few months, so again, I was there when the girls were born, not in the delivery room but in the nursery afterward.

The twins' birth was scarier than Brendan's because as I watched through the glass doors, I could see that both girls were both slow to breathe on their own. Gabby was born first, and after they resuscitated her, they went to Caitlyn. But then Gabby stopped breathing and needed more resuscitation, not an easy thing to watch. I thought I was going to need resuscitation myself, but after the initial scare, they both stabilized.

Again, I had the privilege of being an integral part in the girls' early lives—more out of necessity since having three kids under three, especially with a pistol like Brendan, wasn't a picnic. It was trial by fire since Todd had to go back to Moffit Cancer Center to finish up, so it was Elise and me for the first few months.

In those first few weeks, there was a slight crisis. Elise ended up having to be readmitted to the hospital for a few days to receive IV antibiotics for a serious infection. There I was with Brendan, two infants, and a freezer full of breast milk. I didn't sleep much and lived in the same sweats for three days, but I survived. When Elise came home by taxi, and I opened the front door, her first words were, "You look like hell!" She didn't look so great either, but she was a sight for sore eyes. I was so glad I was there for her, but I couldn't wait to get back to work to rest.

My Real Dream Job Finally!

Work wasn't really rest, but I don't think I could've created a more perfect work environment for myself for the last fifteen years of my career.

Ellen and I had what I would call "the ideal professional relationship" in that we trusted and respected each other. From my perspective, we were a strong team but each with different strengths. She would sometimes ridicule my use of theoretical management strategies or tools, but then again, sometimes she would listen. She knew that if there was a strategic or operational goal I was responsible for managing, it would happen. We didn't always agree, but if I were persistent with a logical argument and had at least some data to support it, she'd finally say, "Fine, do what you want." It was just what I was hoping to hear.

I clearly remember sitting in her office at one of our weekly meetings when I'd catch her up on what was going on.

"Listen," she said, "there are agencies making a ton of money from Medicaid doing fifteen-minute visits with mental health patients to just set up their meds. They're in and out; they can do ten to fifteen visits a day."

I knew she wasn't going to be happy with my response. I understood that the fiscal stability and bottom line of the agency was critical, but I had to say, "Ellen, I don't think that's quite ethical." (I think at that point, she said something like "You think too much.") Then I added, "I can't imagine the state won't get wise to it. I really can't support that. I will talk with my directors, but I'm thinking we want to pass on it."

Of course, the directors thought it wasn't the right thing either, so we never did it. Ultimately the state realized what was happening and not only stopped it, but also imposed financial penalties on the agencies who participated. There weren't many important initiatives we disagreed on, but that one we did, and she was glad I didn't succumb. The next five years that we worked together were much less gut-wrenching and more satisfying. Still, no matter what, I loved my job and never dreaded going to work, ever. Dating and relationships were a different story.

Chapter 19

Dating—The Untoward Affair

It was 3:00 a.m. Joel had come down to get a drink of water and was standing at the sink naked with his back to me and my estrogen patch stuck to his butt.

I didn't laugh then, but I've laughed about it after the fact every time I've the story to a select group of nonjudgmental friends who had never met him and could never understand how I got into that mess or why I stayed in it so long.

That morning, he didn't know I was behind him, fully dressed and ready to run. How could he ever anticipate that?

It had been a wicked hot summer evening, so earlier that night, we had swum in his condo pool after the posted hours. (I don't think there was any arbitrary rule he hadn't intentionally broken at least once while I knew him.)

When a few nosy neighbors heard us, turned on their lights, and looked out their windows, he gave them the finger like a twelve year old. When we went back to the condo, we had sex. It wasn't good for me—my head was not in a good place—but it must have been quite strenuous to transfer the patch from my belly to his butt.

That morning, to his naked back I said, "Joel, I'm going home."

He jumped and turned. "Jesus! Honey, you scared me. Why are you leaving? It's 3:00 a.m. Come back upstairs."

"No, I'm leaving."

Without another word, I went out the door and drove home in my 1979 BMW with the top down and the Adam Lambert song, "Whaddya Want from Me" blaring.

How did this happen to me again? What was wrong with me? When I think back, I had decided I didn't want to be married again. I felt that in a marriage you had to not only compromise on things but also compromise yourself, and I did not want to do that again. I did that twice. That may come off as if I weren't happy in those marriages. That's the weird part; in the moment, I was. Moreover, if you had asked any of my friends or family if they thought I was happy and satisfied during both of my marriages, they would have said emphatically yes. They would have added that they were shocked when I got divorced.

I thought I just wanted a simple relationship with occasional dinners, movies, dates, and sex when I wanted it. Today, they call it "friends with benefits." I didn't need a man to support me. I had good friends, a supportive family, and the respect of business associates. That's what I wanted—a friend with benefits—but I got more than I bargained for with Joel, and I couldn't find my way out.

I could blame the internet, but all the decisions after I had made the connections on Match.com were mine. It all started quite innocently with Joel: a few emails back and forth, then a few phone calls. Conversation was easy. He was an educated, successful financial planner, divorced, with grown kids. He liked to golf, played the piano, and cook. It all sounded quite harmless. We decided to make a date to see a movie, *Crouching Tiger, Hidden Dragon.* It was a weird, Chinese-made film, and he casually mentioned he had a Chinese woman friend. I didn't think twice about that then. I thought he was kind of weird too. He was tall, thin, and attractive, maybe not handsome but certainly engaging. After the movie, which he also thought a little weird, he asked if I wanted to go for coffee. For the life of me, I can't remember why I said, "Thanks, but no." Driving home, I thought the whole thing was strange and had no intention of seeing him again—and I shouldn't have.

Again, I will blame it on those evil, boring Sundays when you're alone. Weeks later, the kids were with their father, and I was bored. Sometimes I make questionable decisions when I'm bored. I hadn't seen Joel since the movie, and I decided to call him.

"I never expected to hear from you again," he said when he heard my voice.

"Well, here I am," I replied.

We talked for a while, and then he said, "Why don't you come to my place? We can talk here, and I'll make you dinner." *Said the spider to the fly!*

His condo was in a gated community, a gate I went through so quickly once on the way out that I broke it. His home was very comfortable, with Crate and Barrel furniture, high-end appliances, and a beautiful Steinway piano in a corner of the great room. The place was absolutely spotless. He did make dinner—chicken, or maybe salmon. I can't remember. Even more scary, I can't remember if I allowed myself to be seduced that night or on a subsequent night. I want to think that I was slightly more disciplined and reserved than that, but again, I was really bored and probably horny (yes, at age sixty!). It doesn't really matter what night it happened. He seemed to know what he was doing, which at the time seemed nice. I didn't realize he knew what he was doing because he had done it so many times before with so many different women.

For about a year, I had made the trip from Waterbury to New Haven probably three times a week to stay overnight with him. I'd leave in the morning and go to work in Hartford, a god-awful commute. When I wasn't with him or working, I was on the road.

We spent many evenings and most weekends together, mostly in New Haven, his neck of the woods, where he had a financial/insurance business. We never had dinner with friends, neither mine nor his. When he and I first met, he told me he was a misanthrope and didn't have any friends, and he wasn't kidding. I remember once saying, as we were getting to know each other, that in relationships I tend to do what the other person wants or at least what I perceive the other person wants. (I didn't add, "And then I seem to make it what I want.") His response was, "Honey, that's not good." Of course, he was right.

When I stayed there, I went to bed early and got up at 5:00 a.m. to walk or run with him along the West Haven shoreline before I went to work. (Did I mention that I hate to go to bed and put it off until at least 11:00 p.m. or later if I don't have to get up?) On the weekends, we went to the Yale Club in the mornings, to use the sauna, where you felt slimy and hot (ugh!), and then had breakfast there before going to a market or *schmie* (Jewish for "shopping around, not buying anything) at Costco or an outlet store. (Did I mention that I hate to shop?) We did a lot of golfing, again always in his neck of the woods, and then usually went back to his place where he would make dinner. We rarely, maybe once or twice, went out to dinner, and we never shared a cocktail hour. He didn't drink. (Did I mention I love to have a cocktail and sit at a bar for happy hour food?) I guess you're getting the picture.

There were many signs that this would not end well. I learned over the year that he didn't get along with his kids. His daughter wouldn't pick up the phone when he called, and he was only in contact with one son. We did visit two of his children—one was an unannounced visit in Charlotte, North Carolina, where his daughter wouldn't allow him to take his granddaughter to the park unless I went. Puzzling! That doesn't happen for nothing.

He was open about his "escapades," which is the only way I can describe them. They included cheating on his wife on their honeymoon, hiding money so he wouldn't have to pay a lot of alimony, excursions to the Bahamas to a friend's house whose wife would meet him at the door naked. There's more to that story, but I'll skip it. The Chinese friend he had mentioned to me was a woman he had a relationship with for years and years. She waited on him hand and foot, was devoted to him and depended on him, and remained heartbroken when he essentially ended the relationship. All these warning signals, yet I stayed stuck in this relationship—until one Saturday when he called and said, "Honey, let's take a little break."

"A little break? What does that mean?"

"I just need some space."

There's not much to say in response to that but, "Okay."

I was caught off guard.

But then I was stalked.

Stalked may be too strong a word. It makes me sound like a victim, and that wouldn't be the whole truth, but I don't think I'll tell the whole truth. When I think about the whole truth, I get stomach pains from the cortisol response that's talked about so much these days as causing illness. Probably for a six-month period, there was stalking, but it went back and forth.

The "break" didn't last. It wasn't long before he called, and we began seeing each other again, but something was very different. There were signs that I wasn't the only woman currently in his life: personal stuff in the bathroom that wasn't his and not mine. Times when I called late and there was no answer, but I knew he was home because he never stayed up or out past 10:00 p.m. I was becoming obsessed with proving myself right. *Who's he with? What's he doing?*

More than once, I drove to New Haven, sat outside his darkened condo, saw her car was parked in his driveway, called him, and left a message that I was there and knew he was with someone.

This complete craziness was beginning to make me sick. I lost weight, had vague abdominal pains, pain and numbness on the right side of my head, swelling and pain in my hands. When he finally "explained" by saying, "Honey, she's just a friend. What's wrong with that? She sleeps here because we run early in the morning," I would stop seeing him, but then I would weaken, and it would start all over. I knew the stress was causing my physical symptoms, but I refused the tranquilizers the doctor offered when all the tests were negative. I was going to handle this myself, one way or another. I had gotten myself into another personal mess. Bad boys.

At this point, I was vice president of operations, functioning at a high level of responsibility and decision-making, moving from one challenging problem to the next, and needing to fully concentrate every hour of every workday.

How did I do it? Compartmentalization isn't always a bad thing. Men's brains tend to be more able to compartmentalize their feelings and be more task-focused, while women's brains have more connections and more cross signals, so they tend to see and feel more than the male brain. I was able to compartmentalize like a man, putting my feelings and emotions aside and fully functioning at work so no one noticed or knew what was going on in my personal life. If they did, they didn't say. My secretary and my boss knew there was a Joel who would call, but that's all they knew. At this stage, I had six senior managers reporting to me who were responsible for clinical operations in seven branch offices, quality assurance and education, Information Technology, and building management. My boss, Ellen, managed finance, human resources, and the board of directors. That was okay with me. It was a stimulating challenge, and I loved it. But I didn't love my personal life so much right then.

I knew I needed to get unstuck, step-by-step. He persisted, "Honey, can't we just be friends and golf occasionally?" I got better at ignoring his phone calls and not responding to his emails, and I finally blocked him. If I started to weaken in the evening, I'd throw my coat on and walk in rain, sleet, or snow until I tired myself out. I made plans with my dear friends, who knew bits and pieces but never the whole bizarre story. It made Joel crazy. When he got crazy, I finally got calm and found my resolve.

The last time I heard his voice was on my answering machine, "Honey, I want to go to Boca for a week. Please come with me. I miss you. We can golf and have a good time. Call me back, please." I didn't.

About a week later, my secretary came into my office. "Nancy, Joel's son Peter is on the phone. Do you want to talk to him?"

I had met Peter and his wife when we had visited them in New York, but I couldn't think of one reason he would be calling me.

"Yes, Jane. Put him through."

"Hi Peter, how are you?"

"Nancy, I have some bad news. My father was hit by a car and killed crossing an intersection in Boca yesterday. They were trying to cross at a busy time, and the sun was blinding. The woman with him hesitated, but he stepped into the street and was hit by a young man who said he was blinded by the sun."

I knew exactly where they were because I had gone to Boca with Joel. They were crossing the street to go to a bagel shop that had the best bialys (similar to bagels) in Boca. And no, Joel wouldn't hesitate to cross the street because he would expect traffic to stop for him. Peter said the poor woman with him was beyond consolation. I knew who it was: Jean, the woman who had worked for Joel and with whom he had a relationship with before, during, and after me. She was the woman who lived one street down from me in Waterbury; the poor woman who could not get unstuck, could not break the hold that a manipulative, narcissistic man like Joel can create for women like us.

Peter called me with the arrangements. I was thankful my daughter said she would come with me. She knew most of the story, but not all. The one time she met Joel, her words were, "He's a freak." My daughter doesn't fall for bad boys. The service was packed with family, friends of family, business associates, an ex-wife, a heartbroken Chinese woman, and a collection of women "friends," including me. I could recognize the women "friends." They were well-dressed, attractive, appropriately sad, but they also looked somewhat relieved.

A few people spoke of Joel, his business acumen, his tennis and golf skills, his idiosyncrasies, and his marching to a different drummer. He would've been surprised at the number of people there—not necessarily pleased but surprised. He had called himself a misanthrope, and he was in every sense of the word. This will not sound nice: I knew I was finally free of Joel, and his death permanently closed the door, a door I'm not sure I wouldn't have left ajar.

I am going to state in no uncertain terms that I cannot find, develop, or maintain a normal personal relationship with the male species. I'm sure it's my issue, and I have no desire to work on it. So there.

Bad Boys in Good Boys' Clothes

After the fiasco with Joel, I avoided the dating scene until unforeseen circumstances presented what seemed like a harmless, random reacquaintance.

My mother and father stayed together for the rest of their lives. I should reword that: They lived in the same house for the rest of their lives, only speaking when they had no choice or when we were all together for celebrations. On their fiftieth wedding anniversary, my mother said she was married for fifty years and added that my father said he was only married for ten.

The family at Mom and Dad's fiftieth anniversary

He always complained to me about her smoking, playing bingo, going to the casino, and spending money. She complained to me about his controlling the TV, drinking too much when he mowed the lawn or used the snowblower, even though we both knew that with so much arthritic pain, it was the only way he could manage it. He occasionally called me to take him to the ER, like the time he nearly cut off his thumb cleaning snow out of the running snowblower. My parents both passed away in their eighties with little suffering and having enjoyed their children, grandchildren, and a great-grandchild. All their grandchildren had unforgettable individual experiences with them and reminisce about them whenever they get together.

But back to dating.

As I got out of the car at the funeral home the morning of my mother's funeral, I heard a male voice say, "I'll be darned, Nancy! Nancy Descoteaux!"

I hadn't been Nancy Descoteaux for forty years, so that got my attention. Then, a tall, thin, handsome guy in an expensive, well-fitting suit walked over to me, and I knew who it was immediately.

"Dickie White!" I exclaimed. "Hi! How are you?"

As he took my hand, he chuckled. "No one has called me Dickie for fifty years." Then he added, "I'm good, good. I'm so sorry about your mother. She was quite a lady. You look great."

I can't imagine that I looked great. I had been crying for days.

"Yes, she was a great lady, and thanks."

At that point, my daughter said, "Come on, Mom. We have to get inside."

But he hadn't let go of my hand.

We saw each other over the next few days during the services. I learned that after he retired as an engineer from AT&T, he helped out part-time at the funeral home owned by friends. He was perfect for it. He was socially engaging, looked more than presentable in custom-made suits, and could drive a limo.

I remembered him well. Growing up, he lived next door to us in a three-family house on the corner. It was Mr. Potle's house, the scary guy who never opened his door on Halloween—as if anyone would want him to. Dick was seven years older than me and gorgeous, so as a teenager, I happened to notice him and often daydreamed that he found me irresistible. As I walked down the walk that ran along his yard from the back of my house to the front, he'd be in his yard, throwing a ball with his brother or mowing the lawn. I was fully developed at twelve years of age and was used to some men—many, actually—leering at me, especially in the summer when I always wore short shorts. I was oblivious to looking "sexy," but even at twelve, I could sense the wrongfulness of the looks. If you ask me, the Me-Too Movement could include every woman born and not be far off.

The seven-year gap between us was too big to close as kids, even though we went to the same parochial elementary school. When I was in third grade, he was already in high school winning athletic awards, and then he went off to West Point. As you can see, he really was just a daydream.

But about a week after we buried my mother, he called, and I can't say I was surprised. I knew he was divorced because (now it gets complicated) he had married a very beautiful nurse I knew professionally. She worked for a Portuguese surgeon I had also worked with in the operating room. The wedding was one of those fairy-tale weddings. Two extremely tall, beautiful, well-known people in the community walked down the aisle of the Cathedral of the Immaculate Conception and vowed to whatever, forever. What's not to love?

Well, this Portuguese surgeon, who, by the way, was about five feet tall and had a Napoleon complex, introduced his very beautiful nurse to a very wealthy, politically connected older man. She fell in love with him, and off they ran to Portugal, leaving Dick behind. It was a big scandal in the city, so of course I knew about it, but it meant nothing to me. I was well beyond Dickie White by then.

Now here Dick was on the phone with me, and the conversation was quite easy. We had a lot in common, having grown up in the same neighborhood with all the same people and going to same church and school. We knew almost everything about each other and our families—the good, the bad, and the ugly. Everyone, even the kids, knew who the mean fathers in the neighborhood were, especially when they were drunk. Dickie White's father was one of them. I remember my mother saying his mother was a saint.

I knew that day he didn't call just to talk, which was okay. I was footloose and fancy-free, as they say, and he was nice and fun to be with. He was a perfect gentleman, respectful, thoughtful, and enamored of me. We went to dinner in nice restaurants, took rides to Watch Hill, golfed a few times, and did anything else I wanted to do. Our conversations were always interesting. He enjoyed a drink or two, but so did I. Occasionally he'd have one too many, but so did I.

One Saturday night we went to dinner at a restaurant famous for its prime rib, a good distance from Waterbury. They had a good dance band, and Dick was a good dancer. We ate—or I should say I ate, and Dick drank Manhattans one after another. We danced, but evidently not enough to burn off the alcohol, and by the time we left, he was slurring his words. When I asked him if he was sure he could drive, he said he could, and I believed him. That was a mistake.

Thank God he knew the roads because we were all over them, bobbing and weaving. I'm not sure why I didn't insist on driving, even halfway home. Somehow, we made it off the highway in Waterbury, and by this time, he was going about twenty miles an hour, and I thought we were home free.

As we crossed the overpass by St. Mary's Hospital, I saw flashing lights in the side mirror. *Oh, crap!* Dick pulled over, and the cops pulled up behind us. I knew where this was going. I knew he was beyond drunk. Dick opened the window, and the cop looked in.

"Can I see your driver's license and registration?"

"Sure," Dick replied.

"Have you been drinking?"

"Yah, I had a few."

"Please get out of the car."

In the meantime, I was sitting bolt upright, staring straight ahead, thinking he was in big trouble. They both walked to my side of the car. Another cop got out of the car behind us, and that cop put his finger between Dick's eyes.

"Follow my finger," he said to Dick. Fail.

"Walk away from me, turn, and come back."

Oops. Fail. Then the cop came to my window, and I opened it.

"Is he your husband?"

"No, officer," I replied. "We're on a date. "

"Well, he is impaired; we have to take him in. We're taking him to the Southbury police barracks. Did you have anything to drink? Can you drive his car?"

"I can drive his car. I did have two drinks."

"I'm sorry, Miss, you'll have to take the sobriety tests. Step out of the car." This was a first for me. Thankfully, I passed the eye test and the walk test, despite wearing high heels. Good thing he didn't ask me to say the alphabet backward—I couldn't have done it.

Slightly shaken, I got behind the wheel of Dick's car and drove myself home. I was awakened by the phone at 7:30 a.m. It was Dick.

"I'm so sorry. Can you pick me up? I don't want my sister to know."

Another first: picking someone up from jail. When I got to the barracks, he was standing outside in the custom-made, very wrinkled suit he had slept in, looking ashamed and embarrassed. I stayed in the driver's seat. There was very little conversation as I drove to my house. He knew that was it. There were no excuses.

"Thanks for picking me up. I guess I really screwed up. Can I call you later?"

"I don't think that's a good idea, Dick. Last night never should've happened. You shouldn't have gotten falling-down drunk, and I shouldn't have been stupid enough to let you drive. I've gone this route before. I'm not doing it again."

I got out of the car and went into the house. I had to call my friend Anne and tell her why I was going to be late for golf. Another "Wait until you hear this!" story.

This was Dick's third DWI (driving while impaired) offense, so in addition to a fine, he could be sentenced to jail for thirty days. On the day of his court appearance, I was working at my office in Hartford. It was about noon when my secretary came to the door, looking puzzled, and said, "There's a man on the phone who says he's Dick White's attorney, and it's critical that he speak with you."

What the heck? I told her to put the call through.

"Hi, this is Bill St. John, and we have a little problem. Dick has to pay a fine of three hundred dollars or go to jail for two months instead of one, and they won't take a check, only cash."

I thought, *This is unbelievable.*

Dick's attorney continued, "Could you possibly bring the cash to the courthouse in Waterbury ASAP?"

At the moment, I was in Hartford on Sisson Avenue, but how could I refuse? So, I asked Jane to cancel my next meeting, explaining that an emergency had come up and I'd call her later. And off I went.

It wasn't the last time I saw Dick. He would call me from jail. I could always recognize the call because it was "Will you accept a collect call from New Haven jail?" Another first for me—and a last. The final embarrassment for him was having to ask me to pick him up when his "time" was up, which I did. He was a sorry sight. He persisted with calls, but I was strong this time, even not opening the door when he physically came to my house bearing flowers. I'm attracted to bad boys, even when it seems they're not.

🐝

Chapter 20

Retirement and Reflection

I *finally got smart and realized* that I've lived my best life independent of men and the ties that bind me to them.

Katharine Hepburn once told Barbara Walters in an interview, "I lived like a man; I didn't live like a woman."

Barbara Walters asked her what she meant by that, and Katharine said, "I've done whatever the hell I wanted to and made enough money to support myself, and I ain't afraid of being alone."

I would second that and add, "I enjoy my own company and don't mind being alone, though there are many people I love and who have brought joy, peace, and a world of blessings into my life on a professional level and a personal level."

On a professional level, I was able to celebrate these relationships at my official retirement party in 2008 when I was sixty-seven years old. The Hartford HealthCare System that the VNA was a part of was evolving and becoming more of an influence on how we managed the agency—more focused on profit and expansion. I felt that in my thirty-plus years at VNA, from carrying a bag as a visiting nurse to being vice president of operations, I was able to maintain a focus on patients, their families, and the staff taking care of them. I was content with what I had accomplished and ready to retire and hand over the reins to someone else.

The shoulders I stood on during my career: Linda Boccialetti, who predicted my future, Iona Waterworth, Ellen Rothberg, and Donna Boehm

By then, I was thoroughly enjoying my grandchildren, Brendan, who was a firecracker that lit up my life and Gabby and Caitlyn, beautiful twin granddaughters who warmed my heart. Time was all I had, and I wanted to make the most of it. I didn't know my retirement party was months in the planning. Ellen and I had an executive assistant, Jane, who had studied at Katharine Gibbs Secretarial School in New York City and could handle just about anything with aplomb (I've been waiting for years to use that word!). It was evident not just in her secretarial skills, but also in the artful approach to her work and the professionalism she demonstrated day in and day out. Jane not only knew where the skeletons were buried, but she also knew where every important piece of paper was and could find whatever we were looking for, even if it was something from twenty years ago. You can only imagine how important this was in a highly regulated health-care business. She did everything

Elise and Joe, two of my favorite people

Joy riding with my grandkids, Caitlyn and Gabby with Brendan riding shotgun

from managing day-to-day support to planning huge fundraisers and galas. She organized and coordinated my retirement party along with our public relations person, Joy.

The gold friends I leaned on: Anne, Jo, and Doll

They had asked me to get there early, and as I was walking in, I saw my dear Waterbury friend and tennis partner Kathy Palmieri walking in as well. It still didn't click. "What are you doing here?"

"I'm here for your party." It was at that point I knew this was going to be more than a few close associates. I was welcomed when I walked in by Jane, Joy, and a videographer. They had set up a reception line, and so it began. I must have stood there for at least an hour, welcoming at least sixty people and smiling, laughing, hugging, and crying.

Jane and me

My son had come from Virginia. My sister Kath, her husband, Harry, and daughter Teresa; my brother, Dave, and his wife and children, Rick and Danelle, were there. My daughter and her husband had come and brought my grandchildren, Brendan, five, and Gabby and Caitlyn, three. I had no idea they were coming, but their being there was momentous.

Employees came from every region, Waterbury, Hartford, Cheshire, Glastonbury, and Windsor Locks. There were execs, managers, nurses, therapists, social workers, home health aides, people from finance and IT, educators, board members (current and past), even consultants we had worked with over the years. Not more important but more significant, there were many people I had worked with and coached, some I had even counseled out of a job not right for them who thanked me and who were successful in new roles outside of the VNA. For me, it was a not only a great celebration, but also rewarding reflection of my work and professional life.

Ellen spoke and made fun of my hair, which I had colored and then not colored and then colored and then not colored. She said she never knew who was coming to work—a dark-haired senorita or a gray-haired hag. More people than I ever imagined spoke, and though sometimes it was more like a roasting, it was all true and affirmed for me that I had walked the walk and not just talked the talk.

Ellen and me

I was fortunate they felt that way because a few months later, when the agency decided to convert to a new software system, Ellen asked me if I would come back as a consultant and manage the project, which I did to completion. This conversion was much easier than the first one I did based on sheer determination to make it work; this time I knew what I was doing. I worked for three more

The Waterbury Home Health Aides: Annie Sanders, Hattie Reed, Esmerelda Paul, Ada Davis, me, Mary Marshall, and Ruth Blanchard. The backbone of Home Health Care

years, consulting on various projects and enjoying semiretirement and the flexibility that came with it.

I had been six months "retired" the second time and bored to utter distraction. I was sitting at the kitchen table on a snowy, dreary day in February 2011 when the phone rang. I saw it was my old boss, Ellen.

"Hi, what are you doing?"

"I'm doing absolutely nothing."

Her question was, "Can I pick your brain?"

I thought, *Thank God.*

My response was, "Please, please, pick my brain!"

That's when I came out of retirement again and worked with Ellen, the Hartford HealthCare System, Blue Cross of Connecticut, and system partners' case managers to streamline and enhance the discharge from hospital care to homecare. It was on a part-time basis, so I still had plenty of time for both family and enough challenging work to keep my gray matter stimulated.

Ellen and I had always worked well together. Though our strengths were different, we were always focused on the patient. She was much better than I was at working the system and the politics of the situation, while I could analyze a process and work with the people involved in it to identify wasted ineffectual steps, what it would take to improve them, and develop a plan to implement them. This project was an all-encompassing project involving senior management, staff, and information systems of all the stakeholders. It was right up my alley up to a point, but soon it became clear that some stakeholders held more sway than others.

When Ellen and I were discussing some decisions that had come out of one of the work sessions with the team, I said to her, "These decisions may work for the insurers, but they certainly aren't going to help the patient transition and manage their disease."

Ellen agreed in principle, but her response was not unexpected. "We have to do what the system wants."

I then made what for me was a very easy decision. If it wasn't about doing the right thing, it wasn't worth my doing. I didn't need the money at this point, and I was seventy-two years old, not a bad age to really retire. Ellen understood that it was better for me to walk away since doing the politically correct thing would not work for me. That was eight years ago, and I have no regrets. You rarely have regrets if you're true to yourself—easy to say not so easy to do.

Eighty Years under My Belt

My retirement party had given me the opportunity to acknowledge and thank the people who had supported me in so many ways throughout my career. When I was turning eighty, I decided to give myself the opportunity to celebrate on a personal level with lifelong friends and family.

I planned it for months. I have never minded my age; in fact, every decade for the past forty years, I had given myself a birthday party. Well, that's not completely true: My daughter surprised me on my seventieth with a fun party, comedian and all.

This current one was a big one, beginning my ninth decade. I wasn't going to wait for someone else to plan it, and the house on the lake was the perfect setting for a summer party. Elise and I had moved there four years ago, and I had moved into my new addition two years ago. It was never a plan that we would live "together," and I had never planned to live on a lake, but here we are.

August was always a big birthday month for our family, so there was always a family gathering around the middle of the month. My father's birthday was August 25, my sister Kath, the 13th, my son Joe's the same as my dad's, and mine on the 19th. When the grandkids were little, we always celebrated down the shore where my mother rented a cottage on the beach.

For me, this year was special. I felt so grateful that I had lived this long without major health issues, but I don't think you can live this long without major losses of family and friends. I had experienced the loss of my brother prematurely in one of the worst deaths I have ever witnessed, and as a nurse I had witnessed many. I also lost more than a few friends, both gold and silver. And then there was COVID-19.

The previous eighteen months hundreds of thousands of people had died from this newly unleashed lethal virus, including many people close to my friends and relatives. There was no treatment, no cure, and really no proven knowledge of how to care for those hospitalized. It was a catastrophic period for the world. I watched body bags being loaded into refrigerated tractor trailers because the funeral homes couldn't handle the bodies. Businesses closed, schools closed, people were quarantined, and fear of contagion was a constant companion for everyone. Even in 2021, with vaccines available, I would not have had this party indoors for fear of COVID.

People were just beginning to venture out unmasked. The timing was right for a celebration.

It was like planning a small wedding. I knew I wanted to have it catered, and I wanted to have a band. I wasn't shy about it; I let everyone I cared about know it was in the works. I researched tents, tables, and linens, bands, and bartenders. I had the guest list in my head. Of course, family. Family get-togethers were rare these days, and it always seemed to be to mourn a loss. Everyone seemed to be so busy with their own families and commitments. We didn't even all get together for Thanksgiving or Christmas anymore.

My mother would turn over in her grave if she were alive. Of course, if she were alive, we would never *not* get together. I had thought about all these things and, not to be maudlin, I didn't want the next get-together to be my funeral.

And of course, friends. I accept that we live in a mobile society, and many young people leave their city of origin to seek adventure, a better life, or a career, but you can't beat lifelong friends, the gold friends. My gold friends are the friends I've had for forty years or more. The silver friends have been friends for twenty years or less. I'm not a gregarious person, so I pick my friends for life.

Maybe ten or fifteen years ago, I told a friend who kept insisting I needed to meet this one or that one that I had enough friends. She was persistent and introduced me to a small group of her women friends, and I will be eternally grateful. They are now my dearest friends, so perhaps I needed new friends and didn't know it.

Between family and friends, the guest list totaled about fifty people. All positive people—I consciously decided I would only have positive people at my party. This was easy since I avoid the company of negative Debby Downers. Of course, happy-dappy people aren't my favorites either. I put the guest list together and sent the e-vites. Most RSVPs responded positively. My sister Jerilyn and her husband, Bruce, were coming from Florida, which made me very happy. I told my grandkids that attendance was not optional for them; it was required.

I'm not sure if Joe and Elise thought I was a little crazy, but of course they went along with me. Once I make my mind up to do something, I'm unstoppable. I rented five large white tables and fifty white chairs and bought two large tents. I wanted it to be casual but comfortable. The casual part was the caterer: Frankie's Hot Dogs, a Waterbury fixture that I had used for my sixty-fifth birthday party. I interviewed and hired the band, made up of four older guys who played the oldies and a singer. I was pretty much prepared well in advance, and now I could only pray to the weather gods, hang out the rosary beads, and hope for sunny skies and temperatures under one hundred degrees. Climate change and global warming I could not control.

The day dawned sunny, warm, and humid with a chance of showers. A chance of showers in Connecticut is like the kiss of death on a major outdoor event, and this was a major outdoor event for me. During COVID-19, it was even more threatening because no one wanted to be crammed in a confined area with fifty people, vaccinated or not. My son, Joe, his girlfriend, Alissa, and his gold friend, Tom, and my daughter, Elise, and her friend set up the tents, tables, and chairs. We set up the bar, which was well-stocked with margaritas and old-fashioned fixings and plenty of red and white wines, and the dance floor, which was outdoor carpet over the bluestone patio.

Not an hour later, the sky darkened and opened up, releasing a deluge. Rain came down in buckets, filling the corners of the tents and threatening to bring them down. We all ran around like fools pushing up the corners of the tents with rakes to drain the water off. I didn't panic, though I easily could have, and within an hour the sun broke through, and the skies cleared. The party was on.

As I was getting dressed, my phone binged with a text message from the band leader with profuse apologies that he didn't feel well and had tested positive for COVID-19. This was the life and times during the pandemic. Nothing was guaranteed. All I could really do was adapt, so I asked Alexa to play the oldies. I wasn't going to get crazy, but when I told my daughter, she said she knew a good DJ and would try to contact him. As they say, everything is as it's meant to be, so he happened to be doing a gig locally and said he would come after that, around 4:00 p.m. Perfect!

My whole family was there. My sister-in-law, Jan, and her son, Rick, and his wife, Sherri, and her daughter, Danelle, came, which was a treat. I didn't get to see them much, especially since David had passed three or four years earlier. His passing was too soon, but he lived the life he wanted and would have had it no other way.

My sister Kath, who is a T-shirt expert, bought T-shirts for herself, Jer, and me printed with "Sisters are like stars. You can't always see them, but you know they're always there." My nurse friends, my golf friends, my lifelong friend Anne, her son, Pat, and his wife, Lorrie, my kids' friends, whom I knew for years and loved, were all there. It was spectacular. Everyone mingled, everyone danced and danced—including my neighbor Nate, who I was surprised to see dancing since I thought he had trouble walking. He and his wife, Laura, had no trouble twisting themselves down to the floor.

At every family party, of which there were many, my sisters and whatever men we were attached to at the time sang "New York, New York" in a chorus line. We did it both drunk and sober, and this party was no exception. Well, except for one exception—Bruce was the lone man standing with us. Lucky guy! Kathy's husband, Harry, had passed during COVID-19, and I had gone through a couple of husbands and a few weird relationships and was happy to be single.

The party was everything I could've wished for and one of the nicest things I've ever done for myself—and I've been pretty good to myself over the years. I never waited for someone to buy me flowers, take me to dinner, or buy me new golf clubs. If I wanted them, I bought them. Of course, I said no gifts were allowed, but now I have enough wine to last until my eight-first birthday.

Epilogue

If you decide to write your memoir, I don't want you to be disappointed. Your children will have no interest in it while you're writing it and likely no interest in reading it while you're alive.

At age eighty-two, I've realized that they really aren't that interested in you as long as they think you're relatively happy and healthy. I've said it to myself often, but now I'm saying clearly and loudly. It's not that they don't love you. My children love and respect me; I know that. Over the years, they've made that crystal-clear in writing with cards, notes, letters, and to a lesser degree, verbally. Our children want us to be healthy and happy for sure, but at a certain age, we become irrelevant.

It seems that when we hang around a little too long, their reverence starts to wear a little thin. They still include us in gatherings, family events, and activities. That's awesome, and I truly enjoy the time with my children, but they have their own lives, for which I am so grateful. They both have good lives, though very busy and at times stressful. I'm not complaining; it is as it should be. On the other hand, I know the influence and impact I've had on them and my grandchildren when I was relevant and did work. This was brought home to me in a recent conversation with my eighteen-year-old grandson.

I was driving him and his girlfriend to his dad's house to drop off his father's car. We have most of our conversations when I'm driving him somewhere because he's trapped in the car with me and has no choice but to listen. I try not to waste those moments and make our conversations meaningful. This trip, he initiated the meaningful. He said they were both going back to my daughter's house. When I asked how his girlfriend was going to get home from there, he said he was going to take his mother's new car and check out how fast a four-hundred-horsepower car could go without her knowing it.

"Bud, I don't think that's a really good idea." It was after 10:00 p.m., and his mother was most assuredly asleep.

"I know, I know. I was just joking. That wouldn't be right. If I did that, it would mean I didn't have integrity."

After I caught my breath, I chimed in, "Bud, without integrity you have nothing."

"I know," he said.

So, if Brendan doesn't read my memoir, it doesn't matter because he got the message when I was relevant, and I've realized the person who learned the most from my memoir is me.

The Metanoia: What I Learned

Most of my adult life, I imagined that I was marching to my own drummer. I believe in free will rather than fate and that we ultimately are the result of our individual decisions or nondecisions, whichever the case. That is, I wholly believed it until I started on this memoir-writing journey. As I laid the groundwork of my story and the story of the people who influenced me over the years, I realized, probably unknowingly most of the time, that who I came to be was well-scripted by my environment and the people in it. These days, we would call them influencers, but mine were flesh and blood, not virtual strangers.

Before I thought about writing a memoir, I knew that the role model I had in my mother was a primary influencer. I silently credited her and alternately blamed her for my strengths and weaknesses, my professional successes and sometimes failures, even at times for my personal foibles. I've discovered that my life's trajectory was more complicated than that.

There are those who would say that the women's liberation movement played a part in that trajectory. I respected the movement but didn't feel it impacted my life directly one way or another, although it did open more doors to the professional and business world for women in general. I never felt I would've been more successful if I were a man. By the time the movement was in full gear, I had already had role models, including my father, who taught me with words or by actions what I came to believe—that "being female was either a nonissue or an advantage."

External forces certainly influence our life paths, but my personal belief is that Cleopatra would have been a woman of influence in whatever century she was born. Eleanor Roosevelt would have been a driver of change, and Rosa Parks would've taken her stand now if not then. I don't for a minute think of myself in their league, but I am who I am, and I would have had a similar life path regardless of the century or decade I was born in. Yes, I would've been swimming upstream; yes, I would've met many obstacles; yes, I would've had diversions; and yes, I would've found a way to live an independent, fulfilling life.

I don't worry about relevance anymore. I'm counting on one of my mother's favorite sayings to be true.

"Honey, the apples don't fall far from the tree."

Acknowledgments

I've always believed everyone's life is interesting and complicated and that they have a story to tell. What I didn't know is what triggered them to begin to write it and more important how did they get to the finish line. The COVID-19 pandemic did set the stage for me by eliminating most options for interacting with the outside world and putting me in a situation where all I had was time to fill. I thought I could at least fill some of it with a virtual memoir class via Zoom.

That was the trigger but the finish line was only possible because of Susan Omilian, women's advocate, teacher, published author, and my writing coach. Susan did not allow my inner critic to take over and she never criticized but redirected with thought-stimulating questions. Without Susan's consistent support and positive feedback I would never have accomplished my lifelong dream of writing a book.

I also must thank my sisters, Kathy Zimmerman and Jerilyn Schvenski, for reviewing my manuscript and refreshing my memory when I was unsure if my perception was the same as their reality. And finally my daughter, Elise, who helped me create a physical environment in my home that encourages thoughtfulness and creativity and my son, Joe, who provides intellectual and emotional support of my story without judgment.

231

About the Author

Nancy Descoteaux Culos is a lifelong resident of Connecticut and currently lives in West Hartford, sharing a home with her daughter Elise Alekshun, a Registered Physical Therapist, and three grandchildren, Brendan, Gabby, and Caitlyn. Frequent visits from her son, Joe Massicotte, an attorney in Washington, D.C. to the Woodridge Lake house add to the good vibe and positive energy.   She now enjoys the simple pleasures of life with friends and family: yoga, reading, writing, walking and working on her golf game, an endless quest.